VEST POCKET

Rhyming

Dictionary

VEST POCKET

Rhyming

Dictionary

of

ONE AND TWO SYLLABLE

RHYMES

by

LANGFORD REED

Copyright 1955 by I. & M. Ottenheimer

OTTENHEIMER: Publishers
Baltimore 15, Md.

Printed in U. S. A.

PREFACE

There is no other rhyming dictionary in the English language that can be regarded as being complete.

You will find that this book is divided into two parts—one-syllable rhymes (words of one syllable or more that rhyme on the last syllable only and are accented on that syllable) and two-syllable rhymes (words of two syllables or more that rhyme on the last two syllables and are accented on the next to last syllable) to give you a complete guide to rhyming.

Also you will see that slang words and geographical names have been included to make this book the one complete rhyming dictionary.

Just to show you how this book helps in completing a rhyme, we offer this limerick that was dashed off on the spur of the moment:

There was a young man known as Joe,
Who was writing a poem for his Flo.
   He wanted a word
   That rhymed with "I heard,"
And this book put an end to his woe.

PART I

ONE SYLLABLE RHYMES

ONE-SYLLABLE RHYMES

A, AH

Ah	baa	bah	blah
ha	la	ma	pa
Shah	ta	faux-pas	holla
hurrah	mama	papa	algebra
cinema	fistula		

(And many other false rhymes ending in "a," such as "America," "Corsica," etc.)

AB

abb	blab	cab	crab
dab	drab	gab	grab
jab	Mab	nab	scab
slab	stab	tab	confab
Punjab			

ABE

Abe	babe	astrolabe
		outgrabe
		(Lewis Carroll)

AC, ACK

bac	back	black	cack
clack	claque	crack	hack
jack	Jack	knack	lac
lack	"mack"	Mac	pack
plaque	quack	rack	sac
sack	shack	slack	smack
snack	stack	tack	thwack
track	whack	wrack	yak
aback	alack	almanac	Appotomac
attack	bric-a-brac	cardiac	demoniac
drawback	gimcrack	haversack	horseback
hyperchondriac	knapsack	maniac	ransack
Sarawak	stickleback	zodiac	

11

ACE, ASE

ace	base	bass	brace
case	chase	dace	face
grace	Grace	lace	mace
pace	place	plaice	race
space	Thrace	trace	abase
bullace	debase	deface	disgrace
displace	efface	embrace	grimace
horse-race	interlace	interspace	market-place
misplace	outface	outpace	populace
replace	retrace	staircase	transplace
uncase	unlace		

ACH, ATCH

batch	catch	hatch	latch
match	patch	ratch	scratch
slatch	snatch	thatch	attach
dispatch	detach	unattach	unlatch

(For rhymes to "watch," see OTCH.)

ACHE (see AKE)   ACK (see AC)

ACT

act	fact	pact	tact
tract	abstract	attract	cataphract
cataract	co-act	compact	contact
contract	counteract	detract	distract
enact	epact	exact	extract
impact	infract	overact	protract
react	refract	retract	retroact
subtract	transact		

(Extend ACK for "blacked" and other preterites.)

AD

ad	bad	brad	cad
chad	clad	dad	fad
gad	glad	had	lad
mad	pad	plaid	sad
shad	Bagdad	bedad	footpad
ironclad	olympiad	monad	nomad

(For rhymes to "wad," "squad" and "quad," see OD.)

ADE, AID

aid	bade	blade	braid
cade	fade	glade	grade
jade	lade	laid	made
maid	neighed	paid	plaid
raid	shade	skaid	Slade
sleighed	spade	stade	staid
they'd	trade	wade	weighed
abrade	accolade	afraid	ambuscade
arcade	balustrade	barricade	Belgrade
blockade	brigade	brocade	cannonade
cascade	cavalcade	citigrade	cockade
colonnade	comrade	crusade	decade
degrade	dissuade	enfilade	escalade
esplanade	evade	fusillade	gasconade
grenade	housemaid	invade	lemonade
marmalade	masquerade	mermaid	nightshade
okayed	orangeade	overlade	overlaid
palisade	parade	pasquinade	persuade
pervade	plantigrade	renegade	retrograde

12

serenade	stockade	underlaid	unlade
unlaid	unmade	unpaid	upbraid
waylaid			

(Also "flayed," "grayed," and many other preterites of verbs ending in AY and EY, which see.)

ADGE

badge	cadge	fadge	**Madge**

ADZE

adze (see plurals of words in AD)

AFE

chafe	Rafe	safe	**waif**
unsafe	vouchsafe		

AFF

gaff	Taff	autograph	behalf
carafe	cenotaph	cinematograph	distaff
epitaph	giraffe	Llandaff	paragraph
phonograph	photograph	riff-raff	telegraph
seraph			

AFT

aft	chaffed	craft	daft
draft	draught	graft	haft
Kraft	laughed	quaffed	raft
shaft	staffed	"straffed"	waft
abaft	autographed	cinematographed	handicraft
paragraphed	photographed	telegraphed	understaffed

AG

bag	brag	crag	dag
drag	fag	flag	gag
hag	jag	knag	lag
nag	quag	rag	sag
scrag	shag	slag	snag
stag	swag	tag	wag
zigzag			

AGE

age	cage	Drage	gage
gauge	page	rage	sage
stage	swage	wage	assuage
disengage	greengage	presage	

(And nearly 100 false rhymes in words ending in AGE in which the final syllable is not accentuated, such as "sausage," "advantage.")

AGUE

Hague	plague	Prague	vague

AID (see ADE)

AIL, ALE

ail	ale	bail	bale
brail	dale	fail	flail
frail	gale	Grail	hail
hale	jail	kail	kale
mail	male	nail	pail
pale	quail	rail	sail
sale	scale	shale	snail
stale	swale	tail	tale
they'll	trail	vale	veil
wale	whale	wail	Yale
assail	avail	bewail	blackmail

13

bobtail	countervail	curtail	detail
entail	exhale	farthingale	female
impale	inhale	nightingale	prevail
regale	retail	travail	unveil
wagtail	wassail	wholesale	

AIM, AME

aim	blame	came	claim
dame	fame	flame	frame
game	lame	maim	name
same	shame	tame	acclaim
became	declaim	defame	disclaim
exclaim	inflame	overcame	nickname
proclaim	reclaim	surname	

AIN, ANE

ain (Scotch)	bane	blain	brain
Cain	cane	chain	crane
Dane	deign	drain	fane
fain	feign	gain	grain
Jane	lain	lane	main
Maine	mane	pain	pane
plain	plane	rain	reign
rein	sane	Seine	skein
slain	Spain	sprain	stain
strain	swain	thane	train
twain	vain	vane	vein
wain	wane	abstain	airplane
again	amain	appertain	arraign
attain	biplane	campaign	chamberlain
champagne	chicane	chilblain	cocaine
complain	constrain	contain	detain
disdain	distrain	domain	Elaine
enchain	engrain	entertain	entrain
explain	fountain	germane	henbane
humane	hurricane	inane	legerdemain
Louvain	maintain	membrane	monoplane
mountain	murrain	obtain	ordain
pearmain	pertain	plantain	porcelain
profane	ptomaine	refrain	regain
remain	restrain	retain	sustain
terrain			

AINT

aint	faint	feint	mayn't
paint	plaint	quaint	saint
taint	acquaint	attaint	complaint
constraint	distraint	restraint	

AIR, ARE

air	Ayr	bare	bear
blare	care	chair	Claire
Clare	dare	e'er	ere
fare	flair	flare	fair
gare	hair	hare	heir
glare	lair	mare	mayor
Herr	pair	pare	pear
ne'er	rare	scare	share
prayer	spare	square	stair
snare	swear	tare	tear
stare	there	ware	wear
their	yare	affair	armchair
where	beware	co-heir	compare
aware	commissionaire	concessionaire	corsair
compere	declare	Delaware	despair

14

debonair	elsewhere	ensnare	fanfare
eclair	forswear	howe'er	unfair
forbear	millionaire	mohair	nightmare
Mayfair	repair	unaware	prepare
welfare	whate'er	whene'er	unfair

AIRD

Baird	braird	Caird	laird

(And preterites of verbs in previous list; thus bared.)

AIRN

bairn	cairn	Nairn	

AISE, AYS, AIZE, AZE

baize	blaze	braise	craze
chaise	daze	gaze	glaze
graze	haze	laze	maize
maze	naze	phase	phrase
praise	raise	raze	traits
yeas	ablaze	amaze	appraise

(And add "s" to words ending in AY and EY, which see.)

AIT, ATE, EIGHT

ait	ate	bait	bate
crate	date	eight	fate
fête	freight	gait	gate
grate	great	hate	Kate
late	mate	pate	plait
plate	prate	rate	sate
skate	slate	spate	state
straight	strait	trait	weight
abate	abdicate	abominate	abrogate
accelerate	accentuate	accommodate	accumulate
acerbate	acidulate	adulterate	advocate *(verb)*
aggravate	aggregate	agitate	alienate
animate	annotate	antedate	anticipate
arbitrate	arrogate	articulate	aspirate
cachinnate	calculate	candidate	capacitate
capitulate	captivate	casemate	castigate
celebrate	checkmate	cicurate	coagulate
collate	commemorate	commiserate	communicate
compassionate	compensate	complicate	confiscate
congratulate	congregate	conjugate	consecrate
consolidate	contaminate	contemplate	co-operate
correlate	corroborate	create	cremate
crenelate	cultivate	debate	debilitate
dedicate	delegate	deliberate	demonstrate
denominate	depopulate	depreciate	derogate
detonate	dilate	discriminate	dislocate
dissipate	duplicate	educate	ejaculate
elaborate	elate	elevate	elucidate
equivocate	eradicate	estate	estimate
expectorate	expostulate	exterminate	extricate
fabricate	facilitate	felicitate	formulate
fornicate	frustrate	generate	germinate
gyrate	hesitate	hibernate	illuminate
imprecate	incubate	indicate	ingrate
initiate	innate	innovate	inoculate
instigate	intimate	intimidate	intricate
inundate	invalidate	investigate	irate
irrigate	irritate	lacerate	liquidate
litigate	lubricate	macerate	machinate
magistrate	matriculate	mediate	meditate
migrate	militate	mitigate	moderate

modulate	mutilate	narrate	nauseate
navigate	necessitate	nominate	oblate
orate	ornate	oscillate	oscitate
osculate	participate	penetrate	percolate
perforate	personate	placate	postulate
potentate	precipitate	predicate	predestinate
predominate	premeditate	prevaricate	procrastinate
profligate	propagate	prostrate	reciprocate
recriminate	regulate	reiterate	remonstrate
reprobate	reverberate	ruminate	rusticate
satiate	saturate	sedate	separate
spifticate	stipulate	subjugate	subordinate
suffocate	syndicate	tabulate	terminate
tête-à-tête	titivate	tolerate	translate
triturate	ultimate	underrate	vacate
variegate	ventilate	venerate	vindicate

(And many false rhymes in words ending in ATE short.
Thus "adequate," "effeminate," etc.)

AITH

faith	wraith		

AKE

ache	bake	brake	break
cake	crake	drake	fake
flake	hake	Jake	lake
make	quake	rake	sake
shake	slake	snake	spake
stake	steak	strake	take
wake	awake	bespake	betake
corn crake	forsake	keepsake	mandrake
mistake	namesake	opaque	overtake
partake	snowflake	sweepstake	undertake

AL

chal (*Romany*)	mal	pal	Sal
shall	cabal	canal	Natal

(And more than 100 false rhymes in words ending in AL
in which the final syllable is not accentuated, such as
"animal," "historical," etc.)

AL (*long*)

Transvaal (*and compare* ARL)

ALC

talc	catafalque		

ALD

bald	scald	Archibald	piebald

(And about twenty preterites of verbs ending in ALL, AUL
and AWL, which see.)

ALE (*see* AIL)   ALF (*see* AFF *long*)

ALK, AUK, AWK

auk	balk	baulk	calk
chalk	gawk	hawk	stalk
talk	walk	Dundalk	tomahawk

(Compare ORK.)

ALL, AUL, AWL

all	awl	ball	bawl
brawl	call	caul	crawl

16

drawl	fall	gall	Gaul
hall	haul	maul	pall
Paul	pawl	Saul	scrawl
shawl	small	sprawl	squall
stall	tall	thrall	trawl
wall	yawl	appal	Bengal
baseball	enthral	football	install
Nepal	overhaul	rainfall	snowfall
waterfall	Whitehall	windfall	

ALM, ARM

alm	arm	balm	barm
calm	charm	farm	harm
palm	psalm	qualm	smarm
alarm	becalm	embalm	disarm
gendarme	madame	salaam	

ALP

alp	scalp

ALSE

false	valse	waltz

ALT, AULT

fault	halt	malt	salt
vault	assault	cobalt	default
exalt			

ALVE (*silent L*)

calve	halve

(*Compare* ARVE.)

ALVE (L *sounded*)

salve	valve	bivalve

AM

am	Cam	Cham	clam
cram	dam	damn	drachm
dram	flam	gram	ham
jam	jamb	lam	lamb
mam	pam	pram	ram
Sam	sham	slam	swam
yam	anagram	Amsterdam	Assam
Rotterdam	Siam		

And many false rhymes, including

bantam	beldam	cryptogram	diagram
diaphragm	epigram	madam	monogram
oriflamme	Surinam	telegram	wigwam

AME (*see* AIM)

AMP

amp	camp	champ	clamp
cramp	damp	gamp	lamp
ramp	scamp	stamp	tramp
vamp	decamp	encamp	

(*For rhymes to* "swamp," *see* OMP.)

AN

an	Anne	ban	bran
can	clan	Dan	fan
flan	khan	Jan	man
pan	Pan	plan	ran

scan	span	tan	than
van	Afghanistan	began	Deccan
divan	Hindostan	Japan	sedan
trepan	Turkestan		

(And about 100 false rhymes in words in which the final syllable is not accentuated. Thus "African," "Puritan," "courtesan.")

ANCE, ANSE

chance	dance	France	glance
lance	manse	prance	stance
trance	advance	askance.	enhance
entrance	mischance	romance	seance

(And about 30 false rhymes in words, ending in ANCE in which the final syllable is not accentuated, thus "ambulance," "vigilance," etc.)

ANCH

| blanch | Blanche | branch | ganch |
| ranch | stanch | carte-blanche | |

AND

and	band	bland	brand
gland	grand	hand	land
rand	Rand	sand	stand
Strand	strand	command	contraband
countermand	demand	expand	reprimand
Sunderland	understand	unhand	withstand
wonderland			

(And preterites of verbs ending in AN, which see For rhymes to "wand," see OND.)

ANE (see AIN)

ANG

bang	bhang	clang	fang
gang	hang	Lang	pang
rang	sang	slang	sprang
stang	tang	twang	harangue
meringue	orang-outang	Penang	

ANGE

change	grange	mange	range
strange	arrange	estrange	exchange
interchange			

ANK

bank	blank	brank	clank
crank	dank	drank	flank
franc	frank	Frank	hank
lank	plank	prank	rank
sank	shank	spank	stank
swank	tank	thank	twank
yank	Yank	embank	disrank
mountebank			

ANT

ant	bant	brant	can't
chant	grant	pant	plant
rant	scant	shan't	slant
aslant	descant	displant	enchant

18

implant	Levant	recant	supplant
transplant			

> *(And about 50 false rhymes by wrongly accentuating the final syllables of such words as "arrogant," etc. For rhymes to "want," see ONT.)*

ANX

francs	Lancs	Manx

> *(And pluralize words ending in ANK.)*

AP

cap	chap	clap	dap
flap	frap	gap	hap
Jap	knap	lap	map
nap	pap	rap	sap
scrap	slap	snap	strap
tap	trap	wrap	yap
entrap	enwrap	kidnap	madcap
mishap			

APE

ape	cape	Cape	chape
crape	dape	drape	gape
grape	jape	nape	rape
scrape	shape	tape	trape
escape			

APES

traipse	jackanapes

> *(And add "s" to above.)*

APH (see AFF)

APSE

apse	lapse	elapse	collapse
perhaps	relapse		

> *(And add "s" to words under AP.)*

APT

apt	rapt	adapt

> *(And preterites of twenty-two verbs ending in AP, which see.)*

AQUE (see ACK)

AR

are	bar	car	char
czar	far	jar	mar
par	scar	spar	star
tar	afar	bazaar	Calabar
Candahar	catarrh	caviar	cigar
debar	disbar	Dunbar	felspar
Forfar	guitar	hussar	Navarre
Zanzibar			

> *(And a number of false rhymes, by wrongly accentuating the final syllables of such words as "popular.")*

ARB

barb	garb	rhubarb

ARCE, ARSE

carse	farce	sparse

(For rhymes to "parse," pluralize some words in AR.)

ARCH

arch	larch	march	March
parch	starch		

ARD

bard	card	guard	hard
lard	nard	pard	shard
yard	bombard	body-guard	discard
petard	regard	reynard	disregard
interlard			

(And extend AR for "barred" and other preterites. For rhymes to "Ward," see OARD.)

ARE (as in "rare," see AIR)

ARF (broad)

dwarf	wharf

ARGE

barge	charge	large	marge
sparge	targe	discharge	surcharge

ARK

arc	ark	bark	barque
cark	clerk	dark	hark
lark	mark	Mark	marque
nark	park	Sark	shark
"Snark'	spark	stark	embark
hierarch	Irak	landmark	matriarch
patriarch	Perak	remark	

ARL, AAL

Basle	carl	Carl	gnarl
marl	snarl	taal	Transvaal

ARM (see ALM)

ARN

barn	darn	"garn!"	Larne
Marne	stern (nautical)	tarn	yarn

ARP

carp	harp	scarp	sharp
Zarp	counterscarp		

ARSE

parse (And add "s" to words in	ras (Abyssinian chief)
AR)	

ARSH

barsh	marsh	moustache

ART

art	bart	cart	chart
dart	hart	heart	mart
part	smart	start	tart
apart	counterpart	depart	dispart
impart	rampart	sweetheart	upstart

ART *(as in "quart," see* ORT)

ARVE

ave	carve	starve	suave
Zouave			

(*Compare* ALVE.)

AS, AZZ

as	has	jazz	"razz"
La Paz			

ASE (*see* ACE)

ASH

ash	bash	brash	cache
cash	clash	crash	dash
fash (*Scotch*)	flash	gash	gnash
hash	lache	lash	mash
Nash	pash	plash	rash
sash	slash	smash	splash
tache	thrash	trash	abash
sabretache	Saltash		

ASH (*as in "wash"*)

quash	squash	wash	musquash

And slang words, as follows:

Boche	bosh	cosh	gosh
josh	posh	slosh	splosh
tosh			

ASK

ask	bask	Basque	cask
flask	Jask	mask	task

ASM

chasm	plasm	spasm	cataplasm
protoplasm	enthusiasm	miasm	phantasm
sarcasm			

ASP

asp	clasp	gasp	grasp
hasp	rasp		

ASS

ass	bass	brass	crass
gas	grass	has	lass
mass	pass	alas	amass
coup-de-grace	cuirass	Madras	morass
repass	surpass	unclass	

AST

blast	cast	caste	fast
gassed	hast	last	massed
mast	past	vast	aghast
avast	bombast	contrast	cuirassed
enthusiast	forecast	iconoclast	metaphrast
outcast			

(*And preterites of verbs in* ASS, *as in "passed."*)

ASTE

baste	chaste	haste	paste
taste	waist	waste	distaste
unchaste			

(And preterites of many verbs in ACE and ASE, as in "based" and "disgraced.")

AT

at	bat	brat	cat
chat	drat	fat	flat
gnat	"gat"	hat	Jat
mat	pat	Pat	plait
plat	rat	sat	slat
spat	sprat	tat	that
vat	acrobat	Ballarat	combat *(verb)*
Herat	loquat	Montserrat	polecat
tit-for-tat			

ATE (see AIT)   ATCH (see ACH)

ATH

bath	Bath	Gath	hath
hearth	lath	math	path
"rath" *(Lewis Carroll)*	scath	aftermath	bypath
Penarth			

ATHE

| bathe | athe | scathe | swathe |

AUB, ORB

| daub | orb | Taube | absorb |

AUD

bawd	broad	Claude	fraud
gaud	laud	Maud	abroad
applaud	defraud		

(And many preterites of verbs in AW, as "clawed." Compare OARD and ORDE.)

AUGH (see AFF)
AUGHT and OUGHT

aught	bought	brought	caught
fought	fraught	naught	nought
ought	sought	taught	taut
wrought	besought	bethought	distraught
forethought	methought	overwrought	

(Compare ORT.)

AUK, AULK and AWK (see ALK)   AUN (see AWN)

AUNCH

| haunch | launch | paunch | staunch |

AUNT *(broad)*

| chaunt | daunt | gaunt | haunt |
| jaunt | taunt | vaunt | avaunt |

AUSE, AUZE

awes	cause	clause	gauze
pause	tawse	applause	because
turquoise			

(And add "s" to certain words in AW.)

22

AV

have	Slav		

AVE

brave	cave	crave	Dave
drave	gave	grave	knave
lave	nave	pave	rave
save	shave	slave	stave
they've	trave	waive	wave
architrave	behave	conclave	deprave
engrave	enslave	forgave	margrave
octave	outbrave		

AW

awe	caw	chaw	claw
craw	daw	draw	flaw
gnaw	haw	jaw	law
maw	paw	pshaw	raw
saw	Shaw	squaw	straw
taw	thaw	yaw	foresaw
cat's-paw	Choctaw	guffaw	jackdaw
macaw	overawe	usquebaugh	withdraw
Warsaw			

AWK (see ALK)   AWL (see ALL)

AWN

awn	bawn	brawn	dawn
drawn	faun	fawn	lawn
pawn	prawn	sawn	spawn
yawn	withdrawn		

(Compare ORN.)

AX

claques	flax	lax	Max
pax	plaques	sax. (for saxo-	tax
wax	borax	climax phone)	parallax
relax	thorax		

(And see AC and ACK and add "s.")

AZ

as	has	jazz	

(And see under AS.)

AZE (see AISE)

AY, EY

bay	bey	bray	Bray
clay	day	dey	dray
drey	eh	fay	fey
flay	fray	gay	gray
grey	hay	jay	lay
leh	may	May	nay
née	neigh	pay	play
pray	prey	ray	say
shay	slay	sleigh	Spey
spray	stay	stray	sway
Tay	they	trait	tray
trey	way	weigh	whey
yea	affray	array	assay
astray	belay	betray	Bombay
cabaret	café-au-lait	cabriolet	convey
decay	defray	déjeuner	delay
disarray	dismay	disobey	display

23

doomsday	embay	essay	gainsay
gangway	hearsay	Herne Bay	heyday
hooray	inlay	inveigh	Malay
mid-day	mislay	Moray	obey
okay	negligée	portray	purvey
relay	repay	replay	survey
Torbay	Tokay	waylay	

(And more than thirty false rhymes, such as "highway,"
"Monday," "popinjay," etc.)

E, EA, EE

be	bee	Cree	Dee
dree	fee	flea	flee
free	gee	glee	he
key	knee	lea	lee
Lee	Leigh	me	"oui"
pea	plea	quay	sea
see	she	ski	spree
Spree	tea	tee	thee
three	tree	we	wee
ye	absentee	agree	A'shantee
bohea	cap-a-pie	chimpanzee	coterie
coo-ee	debauchee	debris	decree
degree	devotee	disagree	Dundee
fricassee	fusee	grandee	grantee
jamboree	jeu-d'esprit	legatee	lessee
licensee	mortgagee	nominee	"on dit"
oversea	Parsee	patentee	pedigree
pharisee	pugaree	recipe	referee
refugee	repartee	Sadducee	settee
squeegee	Torquay	trustee	vendee
vis-à-vis	Zuyder Zee		

(And many false rhymes in words ending in "y"; thus
"history," peremptory," etc.)

EACE, EASE

cease	crease	creese	fleece
geese	grease	Greece	lease
Nice	niece	peace	piece
caprice	decease	decrease	frontispiece
increase	mantelpiece	masterpiece	obese
police	release	surcease	verdigris

EACH

beach	beech	bleach	breach
breech	each	leech	peach
preach	reach	screech	speech
teach	beseech	impeach	outreach

EAD (short, see ED)

EAD (long), EDE, EED

bead	bleed	breed	cede
creed	deed	feed	freed
glebe	greed	heed	keyed
knead	lead	mead	Mede
meed	need	plead	read
reed	screed	seed	speed
steed	swede	Swede	teed
treed	tweed	Tweed	weed
accede	agreed	antecede	centipede
concede	decreed	disagreed	exceed
filigreed	guaranteed	impede	indeed
intercede	knock-kneed	linseed	misdeed
mislead	precede	proceed	recede
refereed	reparteed	secede	stampede
succeed	supersede	velocipede	

24

EAF (*short*), EF

chef	clef	deaf	

EAF (*long, see* EEF)

EAGUE, IGUE

Greig	league	teague	colleague
fatigue	intrigue		

EAK, EEK, IQUE

beak	bleak	cheek	chic
clique	creak	creek	eke
freak	Greek	leak	leek
meek	peak	peek	pique
reek	seek	sheik	shriek
Sikh	sleek	sneak	speak
squeak	streak	teak	tweak
weak	week	wreak	antique
bespeak	bezique	critique	unique

EAL, EEL

creel	deal	Deal	eel
feel	heal	heel	he'll
keel	Kiel	leal	meal
Neal	peal	peel	real
reel	seal	she'll	skeel
squeal	steal	steel	streel
sweal	teal	veal	weal
we'll	wheel	zeal	anneal
appeal	automobile	chenille	cochineal
commonweal	conceal	congeal	deshabille
genteel	ideal	imbecile	profile
repeal	reveal	unreal	

EALD, IELD

field	shield	weald	wield
yield			

(And preterites of verbs in previous list.)

EALM

elm	helm	realm	whelm
overwhelm			

EALTH

health	stealth	wealth	commonwealth

EAM, EEM

beam	bream	Cheam	cream
deem	dream	gleam	ream
scheme	scream	seam	seem
steam	stream	team	teem
theme	abeam	beseem	blaspheme
disesteem	esteem	redeem	supreme

EAMT, EMPT

dreamt	kempt	tempt	attempt
contempt	exempt	unkempt	

EAN, EEN

bean	been	clean	dean
e'en	glean	green	jean

25

keen	lean	lien	mean
mesne	mien	quean	queen
scene	screen	seen	sheen
spleen	teen	wean	ween
yean	aniline	between	bombazine
brigantine	canteen	careen	chlorine
Christine	Clementine	colleen	convene
contravene	crinoline	demean	Doreen
eighteen	Eileen	evergreen	fifteen
fourteen	gabardine	Geraldine	gelatine
go-between	guillotine	intervene	iodine
Jacqueline	kerosene	machine	MacLean
magazine	margarine	misdemean	nectarine
nicotine	nineteen	obscene	overseen
quarantine	quinine	routine	saccharine
sardine	seccotine	serene	seventeen
shagreen	shebeen	sixteen	sordine
spalpeen	submarine	tambourine	tangerine
terrene	tontine	tureen	ultramarine
umpteen	unclean	unforeseen	unseen
vaseline	velveteen	zebrine	

EAND, IEND

fiend (*And preterites of some verbs in previous list.*)

EANT (*see* ENT)

EAP, EEP

cheap	chepe	clepe	creep
deep	heap	jeep	keep
leap	neap	peep	reap
sheep	sleep	steep	sweep
threap	weep	asleep	overleap

EAR, EER, EIR, ERE, IER

beer	bier	blear	cere
cheer	clear	dear	deer
drear	ear	fear	fleer
gear	hear	here	jeer
Lear	leer	mere	near
peer	pier	queer	rear
sear	seer	shear	sheer
"skeer"	smear	sneer	spear
sphere	steer	tear	tier
vere	veer	weir	year
adhere	appear	atmosphere	auctioneer
austere	bandoleer	brigadier	bombardier
buccaneer	carabineer	career	cashier
Cashmere	cavalier	chandelier	chanticleer
charioteer	chevalier	chiffonier	cohere
commandeer	compeer	disappear	domineer
endear	engineer	fusilier	gazetteer
gondolier	grenadier	halberdier	hemisphere
inhere	insincere	interfere	mountaineer
muleteer	musketeer	mutineer	overhear
oversear	pamphleteer	persevere	pioneer
privateer	profiteer	rehear	reindeer
revere	scrutineer	severe	sincere
sonneteer	Tangier	uprear	veneer
volunteer	Windermere		

(*And "Algiers" for plurals.*)

EARCH, ERCH, IRCH, URCH

birch	church	Kertch	lurch

26

| perch | search | smirch | besmirch |
| research | | | |

EARD (short), ERD, IRD, URD

bird	curd	gird	beard
herd	Kurd	sherd	surd
third	word	absurd	administered
massacred	ministered	registered	

(And preterites of many verbs in ER, IR, and UR, which see.)

EARD (long), EIRD

| beard | weird |

(And more than forty preterites of verbs in EAR, EER and ERE, which see.)

EARL, IRL, URL

churl	curl	earl	furl
girl	hurl	pearl	purl
skirl	twirl	whirl	uncurl
unfurl			

EARLED, IRLED, ORLD

| world |

(And preterites of verbs in previous list.)

EARN, ERN, URN

Berne	burn	churn	earn
erne	fern	hern	kerne
learn	querne	spurn	stern
tern	turn	urn	yearn
adjourn	astern	concern	discern
intern	Lucerne	overturn	return
sojourn	unconcern	unlearn	

EARSE (see ERCE)   EART (see ART)

EARTH, ERTH, IRTH

berth	birth	dearth	earth
firth	girth	mirth	Perth
worth			

(For rhymes for "hearth," see ATH.)

EASE (as in "lease," see EACE)

EASE (soft), EEZE, ISE

breeze	Caius	cheese	ease
freeze	frieze	Guise	grease **(verb)**
mise	please	seize	skis
sneeze	squeeze	tease	these
appease	Burmese	cerise	chemise
Chinese	Japanese	Louise	Maltese
Portuguese	Pyrenees	Siamese	trapeze
Tyrolese	valise	Viennese	

(And see EA and EE for many plurals, thus "fleas," "fees.")

EAST, IEST

| beast | east | feast | least |
| priest | yeast | artiste | |

(And preterites of verbs in EACE and EASE, soft, which see. For rhymes to "breast," see EST.)

EAT, EET, EIT, ITE

beat	beet	bleat	cheat
cleat	Crete	eat	feat
'feet	fleet	greet	heat
meat	meet	mete	neat
peat	Pete	pleat	seat
sheet	skeet	sleet	street
suite	sweet	teat	treat
wheat	complete	conceit	deceit
defeat	discreet	discrete	effete
elite	entreat	escheat	incomplete
indiscreet	obsolete	petite	repeat
replete	retreat	secrete	

(For rhymes to "great," see AIT)

EATH (*short*)

Beth	breath	death	saith
Seth			

EATH (*long*)

heath	Leith	Meath	neath
Neath	sheath	teeth	wreath
beneath	bequeath	Blackheath	Dalkeith
underneath	unsheathe		

EATHE

breathe	seethe	sheathe	teethe
wreathe	bequeath		

EAVE, EIVE, EVE, LEVE

beeve	cleave	eave	eve
Eve	greave	grieve	heave
leave	lieve	peeve	reeve
screeve	sheave	sleeve	Steve
thieve	vive	weave	we've
achieve	aggrieve	believe	bereave
conceive	deceive	disbelieve	interleave
perceive	preconceive	receive	relieve
reprieve	retrieve	undeceive	unweave

EB, EBB

bleb	ebb	Feb.	neb
reb	web	Webb	

ECK

beck	check	cheque	Czech
deck	fleck	"heck"	neck
peck	reck	sec	speck
trek	wreck	bedeck	henpeck
Quebec	zebec		

ECT

sect	abject	adject	affect
architect	bisect	circumspect	collect
conflict	connect	correct	defect
deflect	deject	detect	dialect
direct	disaffect	disconnect	disinfect
elect	erect	expect	incorrect
infect	insect	inspect	intellect
interject	intersect	introspect	neglect
object	pandect	perfect	prefect

28

project	prospect	protect	recollect
reflect	reject	respect	retrospect
select	subject	suspect	traject
vivisect			

(And preterites of verbs in ECK, which see.)

ED, EAD (*short*)

bed	bled	bread	bred
dead	dread	fed	fled
Fred	head	lead	led
Ned	pled	read	red
said	shed	shred	sled
sped	spread	stead	Ted
thread	tread	wed	abed
ahead	behead	bedstead	blockhead
bulkhead	gingerbread	instead	loggerhead
misled	trucklebed	unread	unsaid

(Also preterites and past participles ending in ED when the final syllable is accentuated, as in "visited.")

EDE (*see* EAD, *long*)

EDGE

edge	dredge	fledge	hedge
kedge	ledge	pledge	Reg (*for Regi-*
sedge	sledge	veg. (*for vege-*	*nald*)
allege	privilege	*tables*)	wedge
		sacrilege	

| EE (*see* E) | EECE (*see* EACE) |

| EECH (*see* EACH) | EED (*see* EAD) |

EEF, IEF

beef	brief	chief	crief
fief	feof	grief	leaf
lief	reef	sheaf	thief
bas-relief	belief	disbelief	enfeoff
handkerchief	misbelief	neckerchief	unbelief

| EEK (*see* EAK) | EEL (*see* EAL) |

| EEM (*see* EAM) | EER (*see* EAR) |

| EFSE (*see* EASE) | EET (*see* EAT) |

EFT

| cleft | deft | eft | heft |
| left | theft | weft | bereft |

EG

beg	clegg	dreg	egg
keg	leg	Meg	peg
seg	skeg	"yegg"	nutmeg
philabeg			

| EGM (*see* EM) | EIGN, EIN (*see* AIN) |

EL, ELLE

bell	belle	cell	dell
dwell	ell	fell	hell
knell	Nell	quell	sell
shell	smell	spell	swell
tell	well	yell	asphodel

bagatelle	befell	calomel	caramel
citadel	cockerel	compel	Cornell
debel	dispel	doggerel	Estelle
excel	expel	farewell	foretell
gazelle	hotel	impel	infidel
lapel	mackerel	muscatel	parallel
pell-mell	philomel	rebel	repel
rondel	sentinel	undersell	villanelle

ELD

| eld | geld | held | weld |
| beheld | | | |

(And preterites of some verbs in previous list.)

ELF

delf	delph	elf	Guelph
pelf	self	shelf	himself
herself	myself	thyself	yourself

ELK

| elk | whelk | yelk |

ELM (see EALM)

ELP

| help | kelp | skelp | whelp |
| yelp | | | |

ELT

belt	Celt	dealt	dwelt
felt	Kelt	knelt	melt
pelt	smelt	spelt	svelte
veldt	welt		

ELVE

| delve | helve | shelve | twelve |

EM

gem	hem	Jem	phlegm
Shem	stem	them	apothegm
condemn	contemn	diadem	requiem
theorem	stratagem		

("Thames" for plurals.)

EME (see EAM)   EMPT (see EAMT)

EMP

| hemp | kemp |

EN

Ben	den	fen	glen
hen	ken	men	pen
sen	ten	then	wen
when	wren	ven	

ENCE, ENSE

dense	fence	hence	pence
senso	tense	thence	whence
commence	commonsense	condense	defense
dispense	expense	immense	incense
intense	offense	prepense	pretense

(And over 100 false rhymes by accentuating the final syllables of such words as "impertinence," "reference.")

ENCH

bench	blench	clench	drench
French.	quench	stench	tench
trench	wench	wrench	intrench

END

bend	blend	end	fend
friend	kenned	lend	mend
penned	rend	send	spend
tend	trend	vend	wend
amend	append	apprehend	ascend
attend	befriend	commend	compend
comprehend	condescend	contend	defend
depend	descend	discommend	distend
dividend	expend	extend	forfend
impend	intend	misapprehend	misspend
offend	Ostend	portend	pretend
propend	recommend	reprehend	reverend
South End	superintend	suspend	transcend

ENGTH

length   strength

ENS

cleanse   ens   lens

(*Add "s" to words in EN.*)

ENSE (see ENCE)

ENT

bent	Brent	cent	fent
gent	Kent	lent	Lent
meant	pent	rent	scent
sent	spent	tent	Trent
vent	went	absent (*verb*)	accent (*verb*)
acquent	anent	ascent	assent
augment	cement	circumvent	comment
consent	content	descent	dissent
event	extent	ferment	foment
frequent	indent	intent	invent
lament	misspent	present (*verb*)	prevent
repent	represent	resent	unbent

(*And more than 200 false rhymes, by accentuating the final syllables of such words as "penitent," "sapient," etc.*)

EPP

nep	pep	"prep"	repp
skep	step	yep	Dieppe
demirep			

(*Pluralize to rhyme with "Schweppes" and "steppes."*)

EPT

crept	kept	leapt	pepped
Sept.	slept	stepped	swept
wept	accept	adept	concept
except	inept	intercept	overslept
precept	yclept		

ER, IR, UR

blur	burr	cur	err
fir	fur	her	knur
myrrh	per	purr	sir
slur	spur	stir	whir

31

astir	aver	bestir	concur
defer	demur	deter	douceur
infer	inter	occur	prefer
recur	refer	transfer	

(And about 70 false rhymes, by accentuating the final syllables of such words as "arbiter," "forager," etc.)

ERB, URB

curb	blurb	herb	kerb
Serb	verb	ascerb	disturb
perturb	superb		

ERCE, ERSE, URSE

curse	Erse	hearse	nurse
purse	terse	verse	worse
adverse	ammerce	asperse	averse
coerce	commerce	converse	disperse
diverse	imburse	immerse	intersperse
inverse	perverse	precurse	rehearse
reimburse	reverse	sesterce	subverse
transverse	traverse	universe	

ERD (*see* EARD)   ERE (*see* EAR)

ERF, URF

| scurf | serf | surf | turf |

ERGE, IRGE, URGE, OURGE

dirge	merge	purge	scourge
serge	splurge	surge	urge
verge	converge	deterge	diverge
emerge			

ERK, IRK, URK

burke	Chirk	dirk	irk
jerk	kirk	lurk	merk
murk	perk	quirk	shirk
smirk	Turk	work	yerk
Albuquerque			

ERM, IRM

firm	germ	Herm	perm
sperm	squirm	term	therm
worm	affirm	confirm	infirm

ERN (*see* EARN)   ERSE (*see* ERCE)

ERT, IRT, URT

Burt	blurt	cert	curt
dirt	flirt	Gert	girt
hurt	pert	"quirt"	shirt
skirt	spurt	squirt	vert
wert	advert	alert	animadvert
assert	avert	concert	controvert
convert	desert	dessert	disconcert
divert	exert	expert	filbert
Gilbert	incontrovert	inexpert	assert
invert	malapert	obvert	overt
pervert	revert	subvert	unhurt

ERTH (*see* EARTH)

ERVE, URVE

curve	nerve	serve	swerve
turves (pl. of turf)	verve	conserve	deserve
observe	preserve	reserve	subserve
unnerve			

ES, ESCE, ESS

Bess	bless	cess	chess
cress	dress	fesse	guess
less	mess	ness	press
stress	Tess	tress	yes
abscess	acquiesce	actress	address
aggress	ambassadress	assess	caress
coalesce	compress	confess	depress
digress	dispossess	distress	duress
editress	excess	express	effervesce
finesse	giantess	impress	Inverness
lioness	manageress	marchioness	mayoress
nevertheless	noblesse	obsess	overdress
patroness	politesse	possess	prepossess
princess	prioress	profess	progress
prophetess	proprietress	recess	redress
repossess	repress	sheerness	sorceress
success	suppress	transgress	undress

(And about 1,000 false rhymes in LESS and NESS. Thus, "uselessness.")

ESH

flesh	fresh	mesh	nesh
thresh	afresh	enmesh	refresh

ESK, ESQUE

desk	Esk	arabesque	burlesque
grotesque	moresque	picturesque	romanesque
statuesque			

EST

best	blest	breast	Brest
chest	crest	guest	jest
lest	nest	pest	quest
rest	test	vest	west
wrest	zest	abreast	arrest
attest	behest	bequest	Budapest
congest	contest	detest	digest
infest	inquest	interest	invest
manifest	molest	obtest	protest
reinvest	request	suggest	unblest

(And preterites of many verbs in ESS, which see. Also a number of false rhymes in which the accent is not on final syllable, such as "conquest," etc.)

ET, ETTE

ate	bet	Cette	debt
fret	get	jet	ket
let	met	net	pet
set	stet	sweat	threat
vet	wet	yet	abet
alphabet	amulet	bassinet	beset
cadet	corvette	castanet	chansonette
cigarette	coquette	curvet	duet
epaulette	epithet	etiquette	falconette
flannelette	floweret	forget	gazette
grisette	lazarette	leveret	lunette
maisonette	marionette	marmoset	martinet

33

mignonette	minaret	minuet	Nannette
novelette	offset	omelette	overset
parapet	piquet	pierette	pirouette
quadruplet	quartette	quintet	regret
rosette	sarcenet	serviette	sextette
Somerset	suffragette	Thibet	upset

ETCH

etch	fetch	ketch	fletch
retch	sketch	stretch	vetch
wretch	outstretch		

ETE (see EAT) EVE (see EAVE) EUD (see OOD)

EW, IEU, UE (with diphthong)

cue	dew	due	ewe
few	gnu	hew	hue
lieu	mew	new	pew
queue	slew	spew	stew
strew	sue	Sue	view
yew	you	adieu	anew
askew	avenue	Baku	barbecue
bedew	bellevue	beshrew	curfew
curlew	emu	endue	ensue
mildew	parvenu	purlieu	pursue
renew	residue	retinue	review
revenue	subdue	venue	

EW, UE (no diphthong) and OO

blew	blue	boo	brew
chew	clew	clue	coup
crew	Crewe	do	drew
flew	flue	glue	goût (taste)
grew	loo	Lou	moo
rue	screw	shoe	shrew
slew	strew	sou	thew
threw	through	to	too
true	two	who	woo
you	zoo	accrue	ado
bamboo	billet-doux	canoe	cockatoo
construe	cuckoo	debut	entre-nous
kangaroo	misconstrue	Peru	ragout
rendezvous	shampoo	surtout	taboo

EX

cheques	Exe	flex	Rex
sex	"specs"	treks	vex
annex	circumflex	codex	complex
convex	index	perplex	reflex

(Also the present tense of verbs and the plurals of nouns in ECK, as in "decks" and "wrecks")

EZ

| fez | Fez | sez | Les. (for Leslie) |

I (see Y)

IAR

(As in "liar," see two-syllable rhymes.)

IB

bib	crib	dib	drib
fib	glib	jib	nib
quib	rib	squib	

34

IBE

bribe	gibe	gybe	kibe
scribe	tribe	ascribe	circumscribe
describe	diatribe	imbibe	inscribe
prescrib	proscribe	subscribe	superscribe
transcribe			

IC, ICK

brick	chick	click	crick
Dick	flick	hick	kick
lick	Mick	nick	pick
prick	quick	rick	sic
sick	slick	snick	spick
stick	thick	tic	tick
trick	Vic	wick	Wick

And false rhymes as follows:

arsenic	bishopric	candlestick	catholic
caustic	choleric	fiddlestick	heraldic
heretic	impolitic	lunatic	Pickwick
plethoric	politic	rhetoric	

ICE, ISE (short)

bice	dice	ice	lice
mice	nice	price	rice
slice	spice	splice	thrice
trice	twice	vice	advice
concise	device	entice	precise
sacrifice	suffice		

ICH (see ITCH)   ICK (see IC)

ICT

Pict	strict	addict	afflict
benedict	conflict	constrict	contradict
convict	depict	edict	evict
interdict	predict	relict	restrict

(And preterites of verbs in ICK, which see.)

ID

bid	chid	Cid	did
grid	hid	kid	lid
mid	quid	rid	skid
slid	squid	thrid	yid
amid	eyelid	forbid	Madrid
outbid	pyramid	underbid	

IE (see Y)

IDE, IED

bide	bride	chide	Clyde
glide	gride	guide	hide
Hyde	pride	ride	Ryde
side	slide	snide	stride
tide	wide	abide	aside
astride	backside	backslide	beside
betide	broadside	Christmastide	collide
coincide	confide	decide	deride
divide	elide	eventide	fratricide
homicide	infanticide	insecticide	inside
matricide	misguide	noontide	parricide
preside	provide	regicide	reside
subdivide	suicide	tyrannicide	

*(Also "cried," "died," "signified," and about 70 other pret-
crites of verbs in Y, IE and YE, which see.)*

35

IDES

besides   ides
(And add "s" to words in previous list.)

IDGE

bridge	midge	ridge	abridge
cartridge	partridge	privilege	sacrilege

IDST

bidst	chidst	didst	hidst
midst	ridst	slidst	amidst
forbidst			

IEF (*see* EEF)

IEGE

liege   siege   besiege

IEND (*see* EAND)   IER (*see* EAR)

IELD (*see* EALD)

IERCE

fierce	Pearce	pierce	tierce

IEVE (*see* EAVE)

IF, IFF, YPH

biff	cliff	glyph	if
niff	quif	"Riff"	skiff
sniff	stiff	tiff	whiff

IFE

fife	Fife	knife	life
naif	rife	strife	wife

IFT

clift	drift	gift	lift
rift	shift	sift	swift
thrift	adrift	snowdrift	spendthrift
uplift			

(And preterites of verbs in IF.)

IG

big	brig	dig	fig
gig	grig	jig	pig
prig	rig	snig	sprig
swig	twig	Whig	wig
periwig	whirligig		

IGH (*see* Y)   IGHT (*see* ITE)   IGN (*see* INE)

IKE

bike	dyke	hike	Ike
like	Mike	pike	shrike
spike	strike	tyke	alike
dislike	Klondyke	mislike	turnpike
unlike	Vandyke		

IL, ILL

bill	Bill	brill	chill
dill	drill	fill	frill
gill	grill	grille	hill

ill	Jill	kill	mill
nil	pill	quill	rill
skill	spill	squill	still
swill	thrill	till	trill
twill	'twill (*it will*)	will	Will
Brazil	codicil	daffodil	distill
downhill	Evansville	freewill	fulfil
instil	quadrille	Seville	until
uphill	watermill		

ILCH

filch	milch	pilch

ILD (*short*)

build	gild	guild	rebuild

(*And preterites of verbs in IL, as in "billed."*)

ILD (*long*)

child	mild	wild

(*And preterites of verbs in ILE, thus "filed," "exiled."*)

ILE, ISLE, YLE

aisle	bile	chyle	file
guile	I'll	isle	milo
Nile	pile	rile	smile
stile	style	tile	vile
while	wilo	Anglophile	Argyle
Carlyle	compile	crocodile	defile
diastyle	exile	Francophile	domicile (*verb*)
gentile	infantile	juvenile	mercantile
peristyle	puerile	reconcile	revile
servile	tensile		

ILK

bilk	ilk	milk	silk

ILN

biln	kiln	Milne

ILT

built	gilt	guilt	hilt
jilt	kilt	lilt	quilt
silt	spilt	milt	stilt
tilt	wilt	rebuilt	unbuilt

ILTH

filth	spilth	tilth

IM

brim	dim	glim	grim
him	hymn	Jim	limb
limn	Lympne	prim	rim
skim	slim	swim	Tim
trim	Trim	vim	whim
bedim	cherubim	interim	pilgrim
pseudonym	Sanhedrim	seraphim	synonym

IME

chime	chyme	climb	clime
crime	dime	grime	lime
Lyme	mime	prime	rhyme
rime	slime	thyme	time
overtime	pantomime	sublime	

IMES (*pluralize above*) sometimes

I

IMP

blimp	"chimp"	crimp	gimp
imp	jimp	limp	pimp
"simp"	shrimp	skimp	

IMPSE

glimpse   (*And pluralize words in above list.*)

IN, INN, INE (*short*)

bin	chin	din	djinn
fin	Finn	Glynne	gin
grin	in	inn	kin
lyn	Lynn	pin	quin
shin	sin	skin	spin
thin	tin	twin	whin
win	akin	begin	Berlin
cannikin	chagrin	Corinne	culverin
discipline	feminine	finickin	harlequin
herein	heroine	jacobin	javelin
jessamine	kilderkin	libertine	mandarin
mandolin	mannequin	minikin	origin
paladin	palanquin	peregrine	ravelin
wherein	unpin	violin	wherein
within			

INCE

mince	prince	quince	rinse
since	wince	convince	evince

INCH

cinch	clinch	finch	flinch
inch	lynch	pinch	winch

INCT, INKED

tinct	distinct	extinct	indistinct
instinct	precinct	succinct	

(*And preterites of verbs in* INK, *as in* "blinked.")

IND (*short*) *and* INNED

Scinde	wind	abscind	rescind
tamarind			

(*And preterites of verbs in* IN *and* INE, *as in* "pinned" *and* "disciplined.")

IND (*long*) *and* INED

bind	blind	find	grind
hind	kind	mind	rind
wind	behind	gavelkind	mankind
purblind	remind	unkind	unwind
womankind			

(*And preterites of verbs in* IGN *and* INE, *as in* "signed" *and* "dined.")

INE

brine	chine	dine	eyne
fine	kine	Klein	line
mine	nine	pine	Rhine
shine	shrine	sign	sine
spine	Stein	swine	syne
thine	tine	Tyne	trine
twine	vine	whine	wine
align	alkaline	anodyne	aquiline
Argentine	asinine	assign	brigantine
Byzantine	calcine	canine	carbine
carmine	celandine	Clementine	columbine

38

combine	concubine	condign	consign
coastline	countermine	crystalline	decline
define	design	disincline	divine
eglantine	elephantine	enshrine	entwine
feline	incardine	incline	indign
interline	intertwine	iodine	leonine
malign	moonshine	opine	outline
outshine	palatine	porcupine	recline
refine	reline	repine	saline
saturnine	serpentine	sunshine	superfine
turpentine	underline	undermine	untwine
valentine	vesperine	woodbine	

ING

bring	cling	ding	fling
king	ling	Ming	ring
sing	sling	spring	sting
string	swing	thing	Thring
wing	wring	unsling	

*(And more than 1,000 false rhymes in present participles,
as in "happening," "issuing," etc.)*

INGE

binge	cringe	fringe	hinge
singe	springe	tinge	twinge
astringe	befringe	impinge	infringe
syringe	unhinge		

INK

blink	brink	chink	clink
drink	gink	ink	kink
link	mink	pink	prink
rink	shrink	sink	skink
slink	stink	swink	think
tink	twink	wink	zinc
bethink	hoodwink	interlink	methink

INT (short)

dint	flint	Flint	glint
hint	lint	mint	print
quint	splint	sprint	squint
stint	tint	aquatint	asquint
imprint	peppermint	reprint	

(No rhyme for "pint.")

INTH

| plinth | absinthe | Corinth | hyacinth |
| labyrinth | | | |

INX, INKS

| jinx | lynx | minx | sphinx |
| larynx | | | |

(And add "s" to nouns and verbs in INK.)

IP

chip	clip	dip	drip
flip	gyp	grip	hip
kip	lip	nip	pip
quip	rip	scrip	ship
sip	skip	slip	snip
strip	tip	trip	whip
zip	equip	outstrip	tranship

39

apprenticeship	battleship	censorship
championship	citizenship	chaplainship
deaconship	dictatorship	fellowship
guardianship	horsemanship	ladyship
partnership	penmanship	scholarship
sizarship	stewardship	workmanship
	and etc.	

IPT

script   manuscript

(And preterites of verbs in IP, as in "snipped.")

IPE

gripe	pipe	ripe	snipe
stripe	swipe	tripe	type
wipe	bagpipe	hornpipe	linotype
monotype	prototype	stereotype	unripe
windpipe			

IPSE, IPS

apocalypse   eclipse   ellipse

(And add "s" to nouns and verbs in IP, as in "snips.")

IQUE (see EAK)   IR (see ER)

IRCH (see EARCH)   IRD (see EARD)

IRE, YRE

byre	choir	dire	fire
gyre	hire	ire	lyre
mire	pyre	quire	shire
sire	spire	tire	tyre
Tyre	wire	acquire	admire
attire	bonfire	conspire	desire
empire	entire	esquire	expire
grandsire	inspire	perspire	quagmire
require	respire	retire	sapphire
satire	suspire	transpire	

(Compare IAR in list of two-syllable rhymes.)

IRGE (see ERGE)   IRK (see ERK)

IRL (see EARL)   IRM (see ERM)

IRN (see EARN)

IRP, URP

chirp   twerp   extirp   usurp

(Past tense to rhyme with "excerpt.")

IRST, ERST, URST

burst	curst	durst	erst
first	Hurst	thirst	verst
worst	athirst		

(And preterites of verbs in ERCE, ERSE and URSE, as in "coerced," "versed" and "cursed.")

IRT (see ERT)   IRTH (see EARTH)

IS, ISS, ICE (short)

bis	bliss	Diss	hiss
kiss	miss	Swiss	this
wys	abyss	amiss	dismiss
remiss			

And false rhymes, as follows:

analysis	antithesis	apotheosis	armistice
artifice	benefice	chrysalis	cicatrice
cockatrice	cowardice	dentifrice	edifice
elephantiasis	emphasis	genesis	hypostasis
hypothesis	jaundice	liquorice	metamorphosis
metastasis	metropolis	necropolis	orifice
paralysis	parenthesis	precipice	prejudice
prolapsis	synthesis		

IS (long), IZ

biz	fizz	his	is
Liz	phiz	quiz	'tis
viz	whiz	Cadiz	

ISE, IZE

guise	prise	prize	rise
size	wise	acclimatize	advertise
anglicize	apologize	apostatize	apostrophize
apprise	arise	assize	astrologize
astronomize	authorize	baptize	barbarize
bastardize	Belsize	brutalize	canonize
carbonize	catholicize	cauterize	centralize
characterize	chastise	christianize	cicatrize
circularize	circumcise	citizenize	civilize
cognise	colloquialize	colonize	comprise
compromise	congenialize	contrariwise	criticise
crystallize	democratize	demoralize	deodorize
demise	dentize	despise	devitalize
devise	dialize	dichotomize	disguise
disorganize	dogmatize	economize	egotize
emblemize	emphasize	epigrammatize	epilogize
epitomize	equalize	etherealize	etymologize
eulogize	euphonize	evangelize	excise
exercise	exorcise	extemporize	externalize
familiarize	fanaticize	fertilize	feudalize
formalize	fossilize	franchise	fraternize
geometrize	gluttonize	gorgonize	gormandize
harmonize	heathenize	hellenize	humanize
immortalize	imperialize	improvise	individualize
internationalize	italicize	jeopardize	judaize
latinize	legalize	liberalize	likewise
localize	macadamize	magnetize	materialize
mechanize	mediatize	memorize	mercerise
merchandise	mesmerize	metalize	methodize
militarize	mineralize	minimize	misprize
mobilize	modernize	monopolize	moralize
nationalize	neutralize	nomadize	occidentalize
organize	orientalize	ostracize	otherwise
pauperize	philosophize	phlebotomize	plagiarize
pluralize	poetize	polarize	popularize
premise	protestantize	proverbialize	pulverize
puritanize	realize	recognize	regularize
reprise	revise	revolutionize	rhapsodize
romanize	ruralize	sanctuarize	satirize
scandalize	secularize	sensitize	sensualize
signalize	solescize	solemnize	soliloquize

spiritualize	standardize	summarize	atomize
televise	finalise	specialize	sunrise
surmise	syllogize	symbolize	sympathize
synchronize	synonymize	systematize	tantalize
temporize	terrorize	theorize	tranquilize
tyrannize	unwise	utilize	ventriloquize
victimize	visualize	vocalize	volatize
vulcanize	vulgarize	weatherwise	

(Also plurals of nouns in IGH and third person singular of verbs in Y. Thus "thighs" and "tries." See under Y.)

ISH

| dish | fish | Nish | pish |
| squish | swish | wish | |

And false rhymes, such as:

anguish	cleverish	devilish	feverish
gibberish	heathenish	impoverish	lickerish
liverish	willowish	womanish	yellowish

ISK

bisk	bisque	brisk	disk
frisk	risk	whisk	asterisk
basilisk	obelisk	odalisque	tamarisk

ISM

chrism	prism	schism	agnosticism
Americanism	anachronism	anarchism	aneurism
anglicism	aphorism	archaism	atheism
baptism	barbarism	bolshevism	calvinism
capitalism	Carrollism	cataclysm	catechism
catholicism	chauvinism	colloquialism	communism
conservatism	criticism	Darwinism	deism
despotism	dogmatism	egotism	empiricism
evangelism	exorcism	Fascism	fanaticism
feudalism	gallicism	heathenism	hedonism
heroism	hibernism	Hitlerism	hypnotism
Ibsenism	idealism	imperialism	Judaism
laconism	latinism	liberalism	libertinism
magnetism	malthusianism	mannerism	materialism
mechanism	mesmerism	methodism	modernism
nationalism	nepotism	occidentalism	occultism
optimism	organism	orientalism	ostracism
paganism	pantheism	paroxysm	patriotism
pauperism	pelmanism	pessimism	plagiarism
presbyterianism	protestantism	provincialism	puritanism
pyrrhonism	radicalism	rationalism	realism
rheumatism	ritualism	sabbatism	scepticism
Shavianism	socialism	solescism	stoicism
truism	vandalism	ventriloquism	vocalism
vulgarism	witticism	Zionism	

ISP

| crisp | lisp | wisp |

ISS (see IS, short)

IST, ISSED, YST

cist	cyst	fist	gist
grist	hist	list	mist
tryst	twist	whist	wist
wrist	academist	agriculturist	alchemist
amethyst	amorist	analogist	analyst
anarchist	anatomist	apologist	assist
atheist	baptist	beneficed	bicyclist
bigamist	bolshevist	botanist	calvinist

capitalist	casualist	casuist	catechist
chiropodist	chronologist	co-exist	colonist
colourist	columnist	communist	consist
dialist	desist	diarist	diplomatist
dismissed	dogmatist	dramatist	dualist
duellist	economist	egotist	emblematist
etymologist	eucharist	evangelist	exist
exorcist	externalist	fabulist	Fascist
fatalist	geologist	geometrist	hebraist
hedonist	hellenist	herbalist	humanist
humorist	hypnotist	idealist	idolist
imperialist	internationalist	insist	instrumentalist
intertwist	journalist	lapidist	latinist
loyalist	materialist	malthusianist	medallist
memoralist	mesmerist	metallist	metallurgist
meteorologist	methodist	militarist	mineralogist
moralist	motorist	mythologist	nationalist
naturalist	novelist	obstructionist	occidentalist
oculist	opinionist	ontologist	optimist
organist	orientalist	pathologist	pessimist
philanthropist	philatelist	philologist	phlebotomist
psychiatrist	physiognomist	physiologist	plagiarist
pluralist	pianist	pietist	polygamist
protectionist	psychologist	psychometrist	pugilist
pyrologist	pyrotechnist	rationalist	realist
receptionist	religionist	revivalist	revolutionist
rhapsodist	ritualist	royalist	satirist
secularist	schematist	scientist	sensualist
separatist	sexualist	socialist	soloist
spiritualist	suffragist	syncopist	tautologist
telegraphist	telephonist	terrorist	theologist
tobacconist	unionist	ventriloquist	violinist
visualist	vocalist	votarist	Zionist

(And preterites of verbs in ISS, as in "kissed.")

IT, ITE (short)

bit	chit	cit	fit
flit	grit	hit	it
kit	knit	lit	mitt
nit	pit	quit	sit
skit	slit	smit	spit
split	sprit	tit	twit
whit	wit	writ	acquit
admit	opposite	benefit	bowsprit
commit	definite	emit	exquisite
favourite	hypocrite	indefinite	infinite
intermit	intromit	Jesuit	manumit
omit	opposite	outwit	perquisite
permit	pewit	preterite	recommit
refit	remit	requisite	submit
titbit	transmit	unfit	

ITCH

bitch	ditch	fitch	flitch
hitch	itch	lych	niche
pitch	rich	snitch	stitch
switch	which	witch	bewitch
distich	enrich	hemstitch	

ITE (long), IGHT

bite	bight	blight	bright
cite	dight	fight	flight
fright	height	kite	knight

43

light	flight	mite	night
pight	plight	quite	right
rite	sight	site	sleight
slight	smite	spite	sprite
tight	trite	white	wight
wright	write	accite	acolyte
aconite	affright	alight	anchorite
appetite	bedight	bedlamite	benight
biparite	candlelight	Carmelite	chrysolite
composite	cosmopolite	contrite	delight
despite	disunite	downright	dynamite
eremite	excite	expedite	foresight
hermaphrodite	impolite	ignite	incite
indict	insight	invite	Jacobite
midnight	midshipmite	moonlight	neophyte
outright	overnight	oversight	parasite
polite	proselyte	recite	requite
recondite	reunite	satellite	stalactite
stalagmite	starlight	sunlight	Sybarite
theodolite	troglodyte	twilight	underwrite
vulcanite	watertight	weathertight	zeolite
zincite			

ITE (short) as in "definite" (see IT)

ITH, YTH

fifth	frith	kith	myth
pith	sith	smith	with
withe	forthwith	herewith	monolith
Penrith	therewith	wherewith	zenith

ITHE

| blithe | hithe | Hythe | lithe |
| scythe | tithe | writhe | |

ITS, ITZ

| Blitz | Fritz | Ritz | |

(And plurals of words in IT.)

IVE (short)

give	live	sieve	ablative
abdicative	abductive	accumulative	accusative
acquisitive	administrative	affirmative	alliterative
alternative	appelative	applicative	appreciative
argumentative	authoritative	causative	cogitative
commemorative	communicative	comparative	consecutive
conservative	contemplative	contributive	co-operative
copulative	correlative	corroborative	curative
curvative	declarative	decorative	definitive
degenerative	deliberative	demonstrative	depreciative
derivative	derogative	desiccative	determinative
diminutive	discriminative	distributive	emanative
eradicative	executive	explicative	figurative
fugitive	generative	genitive	illuminative
illustrative	imaginative	imitative	imperative
inchoative	indicative	infinitive	inquisitive
insinuative	instinctive	interrogative	intuitive
justificative	lambative	laxative	lenitive
lucrative	meditative	narrative	negative
operative	opinionative	palliative	perspective
persuasive	prejudicative	positive	performative
preparative	prerogative	preservative	primitive
privative	procreative	productive	progressive
prospective	provocative	punitive	purgative

44

putative	recitative	recreative	recriminative
refrigerative	regenerative	relative	remonstrative
remunerative	reparative	representative	restorative
retributive	reverberative	significative	speculative
substantive	superlative	talkative	tentative

IVE

Clive	dive	drive	five
gyve	hive	I've	live
naïve	rive	shive	shrive
strive	thrive	wive	alive
arrive	beehive	connive	contrive
deprive	derive	revive	survive

IX, ICS, ICKS

fix	mix	nix	pyx
six	strix	Styx	admix
affix	cicatrix	crucifix	executrix
intermix	matrix	onyx	prefix
prolix	sardonyx	transfix	

(And plurals of nouns in ICK, as in "kicks.")

O, OW, EAU, OE

beau	blow	bow	co. (company)
crow	do (music)	doe	dough
Flo	floe	flow	foe
fro	glow	go	grow
ho	hoe	Joe	know
lo	low	mow	no
oh	owe	po	pro
roe	row	sew	shew
show	sloe	snow	stow
strow	though	throe	throw
toe	trow	woe	adagio
ago	allegro	although	apropos
banjo	below	bestow	braggadocio
bravo	bureau	buffalo	calico
cameo	chapeau	chateau	cocoa
comme il faut	de trop	depot	domino
dus	duodecimo	embryo	falsetto
forego	foreshow	furbelow	generalissimo
haricot	heigh-ho	hello	Idaho
imbroglio	incognito	indigo	intaglio
memento	mistletoe	mulatto	nuncio
oleo	Ontario	oratorio	outgrow
overgrow	overflow	overthrow	pierrot
Pimlico	pistachio	plateau	portico
rondeau	seraglio	Soho	stiletto
tobacco	torpedo	trousseau	undergo
vertigo	volcano		

OACH

broach	brooch	coach	loach
poach	roach	approach	cockroach
encroach	reproach		

OAD, ODE, OWED

bode	code	goad	load
lode	mode	node	ode
road	rode	strode	toad
commode	corrode	episode	erode
explode	forebode	income	

(And preterites of verbs in O, OW and OWE; thus "toed,"
"towed" and "owed.")

45

OAF

loaf	oaf	

OAK, OKE

bloke	broke	choke	cloak
coke	croak	folk	joke
moke	oak	poke	smoke
soak	spoke	stoke	stroke
toque	woke	yoke	yolk
artichoke	awoke	bespoke	convoke
equivoke	gentlefolk	invoke	masterstroke
provoke	revoke	unyoke	

OAL, OLE, OL, OLL, OUL, OWL

bole	bowl	coal	dole
droll	foal	goal	hole
jole	knoll	mole	pole
poll	role	roll	scroll
shoal	sole	soul	stole
stroll	thole	toll	troll
vole	whole	aureole	cajole
camisole	caracole	champagnol	condole
console	control	Creole	enrol
girandole	girasole	parole	patrol
petrol	pistole	rantipole	

OAM, OME

chrome	comb	dome	foam
Frome	gnome	holme	home
loam	"mome" (Car-	Nome	roam
Rome	roll) tome	aerodrome	catacomb
currycomb	hippodrome	palindrome	

OAN, ONE, OWN

bone	blown	cone	crone
drone	flown	groan	grown
hone	Joan	known	loan
lone	moan	own	prone
roan	Rhône	scone	shown
Sloane	sown	stone	strown
tone	throne	thrown	zone
alone	atone	benison	chaperone
Cologne	cornerstone	depone	dethrone
dictaphone	disown	enthrone	gramaphone
grindstone	intone	knucklebone	microphone
moonstone	ozone	postpone	telephone
undertone	unknown	unsewn	

OAR, ORE

boar	bore	core	corps
door	floor	fore	four
gore	hoar	lore	more
nore	Nore	o'er	pore
pour	roar	score	shore
snore	soar	sore	store
swore	tore	whore	wore
yore	war	adore	afore
ashore	battledore	before	Cawnpore
claymore	commodore	deplore	encore
evermore	explore	forbore	foreshore
forswore	furthermore	galore	heretofore
ignore	implore	matador	restoré

46

sophomore   troubadour   semaphore   spoor

(*Compare* OR *and* OOR.)

OARD, ORED, ORD, ORDE

board	chord	cord	ford
board	horde	lord	sward
sword	ward	accord	harpsichord
record	reward		

(*Compare* AUD.) (*And preterites of verbs in previous list.*)

OARSE (*see:* ORCE)

OAST, OST (*long*)

oast	coast	ghost	grossed
ost	most	post	roast
past	almost	hindermost	innermost
powermost	'nethermost	outermost –	undermost
uppermost			

OAT, OTE

float	boat	bote	coat
note	Croat	dote	float
goat	goat	groat	moat
note	note	oat	quote
ote	smote	stoat	throat
ote	vote	wrote	afloat
anecdote	antidote	assymptote	connote
devote	lifeboat	misquote	outvote
petticoat	promote	remote	table d'hote

OATH, OTH

| oth | growth | loath | oath |
| quoth | sloth | troth | Arbroath |

OATHE

| lothe | loathe | betroth | |

OAX

| oax | hoax | | |

(*And pluralize* OAK, OKE, *as in* "oaks," "jokes.")

OB, OAB

Rob	bob	Bob	cob
ob	fob	gob	hob
b	knob	lob	mob
b	quab	rob	snob
b	swab	throb	yob
angumbob	demob	hobnob	nabob

OBE

lobe	Job	lobe	probe
be	Anglophobe	conglobe	disrobe
obe	Francophobe		

47

OCK

block	bock	brock	chock
clock	cock	crock	dock
flock	frock	hock	hough
Jock	knock	Knocke	loch
lock	lough	mock	pock
roc	rock	shock	smock
sock	stock	padlock	pibroch
hollyhock	Jabberwock	laughing-stock	shamrock
stumbling-block	weathercock		

OCT

concoct	decoct

(And preterites of OCK, as in "locked," "padlocked," etc.)

OD

clod	cod	God	hod
nod	odd	plod	pod
prod	quad	quod	rod
shod	sod	tod	trod
wad	demigod	period	untrod

ODGE

bodge	dodge	hodge	lodge
podge	splodge	stodge	dislodge
hodge-podge			

OE (*see* O)

OFF

cough	doff	off	scoff
shroff	"soph"	toff	trough

OFT

croft	loft	oft	soft
aloft			

(And preterites of verbs in OFF.)

OG, OGUE

bog	clog	cog	dog
flog	fog	frog	gog
grog	hog	jog	log
prog	shog	stog	agog
analogue	apologue	catalogue	decalogue
demagogue	dialogue	duologue	epilogue
incog	monologue	pedagogue	synagogue

OGUE (*long*)

brogue	rogue	vogue	prorogue

OICE

Boyce	choice	Joyce	voice
invoice	rejoice	Rolls-Royce	

OID

Boyd	Floyd	Lloyd	void
alkaloid	asteroid	avoid	devoid
negroid	paraboloid	rhomboid	celluloid

(And preterites of verbs in OY, as "destroyed.")

OIL

boil	Boyle	broil	coil
Doyle	foil	moil	oil
roil	soil	spoil	toil
despoil	embroil	gumboil	Lough Foyle
parboil	turmoil		

(Compare OYAL.)

OIN, OYNE

Boyne	coign	coin	foin
groin	groyne	join	loin
quoin	adjoin	benzoin	conjoin
disjoin	enjoin	purloin	rejoin
sainfoin	sirloin	subjoin	

OINT

joint	oint	point	anoint
appoint	aroint	conjoint	counterpoint
disappoint	disjoint	West Point	

OISE, OYS

froise	noise	poise	Troyes
avoirdupois	counterpoise	equipoise	

(And add "s" to nouns and verbs in OY.)

OIST

foist	hoist	joist	moist
voiced	invoiced	rejoiced	

OIT

doit	quoit	adroit	dacoit
Detroit	exploit	introit	

OKE (see OAK)

OL, OLL (both short)

"coll."	doll	loll	Moll
poll	Sol	alcohol	capitol
extol	parasol	vitriol	

OL, OLL (long), OLE (see OAL)

OLD

bold	cold	fold	gold
hold	mold	old	scold
sold	told	wold	behold

49

cuckold	enfold	foretold	freehold
manifold	marigold	unfold	untold
uphold	withhold		

(*And see OAL for preterites of OAL, OLE, OLL and OWL.*)

OLK (as in "folk," see OAK)

OLT

bolt	colt	dolt	jolt
molt	poult	volt	revolt
thunderbolt			

OLVE

| solve | absolve | dissolve | evolve |
| involve | resolve | revolve | |

OM

bomb	from	pom	"Prom"
rhom	Somme	Tom	aplomb
pom-pom	tom-tom		

OMP

| comp | pomp | romp | swamp |

OMPT

| prompt | romped | swamped | |

ON

Bonn	con	don	gone
John	non	on	"scone" (*Scotch*)
shone	swan	wan	yon
anon	begone	bon-bon	bon-ton
bygone	Canton	Ceylon	dies-non
hereon	Marathon	Narbonne	sine qua non
thereon	thereupon	upon	

(*Compare UN for words of three syllables ending in ON as in "champion."*)

ONCE, ONSE

| nonce | ponce | sconce | ensconce |
| response | | | |

(*For rhymes to "once," see UNCE.*)

OND, ONNED

blond	bond	fond	frond
pond	wand	yond	abscond
beyond	correspond	co-respond	despond
diamond	respond	vagabond	demi-monde

(*And preterites of verbs in ON, as in "conned."*)

ONE (*short as in "one," see UN*)
ONE (*long, as in "tone," see OAN*)

ONG

gong	long	prong	song
strong	thong	throng	tong
wrong	along	belong	ding dong
diphthong	Hong Kong	oblong	ping-pong
prolong	overlong		

ONGUE (*see UNG*)

ONK

bonk	conk	honk	plonk

(For "Bronx," add "s" to above.)

ONT *(short)*

font	want

ONT *(long)*

don't	wont	won't

ONZE

bonze	bronze	"onze" *(French)*

(And add "s" to words in ON, as in "cons.")

OO *(see EW)*   OOD *(as in "blood," see UD)*

OOD *(as in "hood")*

could	good	hood	should
stood	wood	would	babyhood
brotherhood	childhood	fatherhood	Goodwood
hardihood	Hollywood	likelihood	livelihood
misunderstood	motherhood	neighborhood	understood
widowhood	withstood		

OOD *(as in "food")*, EUD, EWED, UDE

brood	Bude	crude	dude
feud	food	lewd	mood
nude	prude	rood	rude
shrewd	snood	you'd	alacritude
allude	altitude	amplitude	aptitude
assuetude	attitude	beatitude	certitude
collude	conclude	consuetude	crassitude
decrepitude	delude	denude	desuetude
detrude	disquietude	dissimilitude	elude
exactitude	exclude	extrude	exude
finitude	fortitude	gratitude	habitude
Hollyrood	illude	inaptitude	incertitude
include	ineptitude	infinitude	ingratitude
interlude	intrude	lassitude	latitude
longitude	magnitude	mansuetude	multitude
necessitude	obtrude	occlude	parvitude
platitude	plenitude	preclude	prelude
promptitude	protrude	pulchritude	quietude
rectitude	sanctitude	seclude	serenitude
servitude	similitude	solicitude	solitude

(See under EW for preterites of many verbs in EW, OO, and UE; thus "hewed," "booed," "subdued.")

OOF

hoof	oof	pouf	proof
roof	spoof	woof	aloof
behoof	disproof	reproof	

OOK

book	brook	cook	crook
hook	look	nook	took
shook	spook	took	"amuck"
betook	"Canuck"	forsook	mistook
nainsook	overlook	overtook	undertook

51

OOL, ULE (when pronounced OOL)

cool	fool	ghoul	Goole
pool	Poole	rule	school
spool	stool	tool	tulle
who'll	befool	misrule	overrule
sporrule	Stamboul		

(Compare ULE, with diphthong, as in "mule." Compare, also, UEL in two-syllable rhymes as in "fuel.")

OOL (as in "wool," see UL)

OOM, UME (when pronounced OOM)

bloom	boom	broom	brougham
coomb	coombe	doom	flume
gloom	groom	loom	plume
rheum	room	spoom	tomb
whom	womb	zoom	Batoum
beplume	dining-room	drawing-room	elbow-room
entomb	Ezroum	hecatomb	Khartoum
sitting-room			

(Compare UME with diphthong, as in "fume.")

OON, UNE (when pronounced OON)

boon	coon	croon	loon
lune	Lune	moon	poon
prune	rune	screwn	shoon
soon	spoon	strewn	swoon
Troon	afternoon	baboon	balloon
bassoon	bestrewn	buffoon	cartoon
cocoon	doubloon	dragoon	Dunoon
eftsoon	eschew	festoon	galloon
harpoon	honeymoon	jejune	lagoon
lampoon	macaroon	maroon	monsoon
musketoon	octoroon	platoon	poltroon
pontoon	quadroon	racoon	Rangoon
rigadoon	shalloon	simoon	typhoon

(Compare UNE with diphthong, as in "tune.")

OOP, OUP

coop	croup	droop	group
hoop	loop	poop	scoop
sloop	snoop	soup	stoop
stoup	swoop	"goop"	troop
troupe	whoop	nincompoop	recoup

(Compare UPE.)

OOR

boor	floor	moor	poor
Ruhr	spoor	tour	you're
amour	blackamoor	contour	detour
paramour			

(Compare URE. Also EWER in two-syllable rhymes. For rhymes to "door," see OAR.)

OOSE (short), UCE, UICE (when pronounced OOSE, short)

Bruce	goose	juice	loose
moose	noose	sluice	spruce
truce	abstruse	occlude	recluse
unloose	induce	introduce	

(Compare UCE and USE with diphthong, as in "puce" and "diffuse.")

52

OOSE (long), OOZE, UES

booze	bruise	choose	cruise
lose	Ouse	ooze	ruse
trews	whose	who's	caboose
enthuse	papoose	recluse	peruse
vamoose			

(*Compare* USE, as in "*fuse*," and see EW, IEU, UE *and* OO *for plurals of nouns and third person singular of verbs, as in* "*pews*," "*adieus*," "*hues*," *etc.*)

OOST, UCED, USED (sharp)

ooost	joust	juiced	loosed
noosed	roost	sluiced	spruced
used	adduced	conduced	deduced
educed	induced	produced	reduced
reproduced	seduced	subduced	superinduced

OOT (short)

foot	put	soot	

OOT (long), UTE (when pronounced OOT)

boot	bruit	brute	coot
flute	fruit	hoot	jute
loot	moot	root	route
shoot	skoot	toot	adjute
cheroot	galloot	overshoot	parachute
recruit	uproot	waterchute	

(*Compare* UTE *with diphthong, as in* "*cute*," "*newt*" *etc.*)

OOTH (short), UTH

ruth	Ruth	sooth	"strewth"
tooth	truth	youth	Duluth
forsooth	uncouth	untruth	vermouth

OOTH (long)

booth	smooth	soothe	

OOVE

groove	hoove	move	prove
you've	approve	disprove	improve
remove	reprove	disapprove	

OOZE (see OOSE)

OP

chop	cop	crop	drop
flop	fop	hop	lop
mop	plop	pop	prop
shop	slop	sop	stop
strop	swap	top	whop
wop	atop		

OPE, OAP

cope	dope	grope	hope
lope	mope	nope	ope
pope	rope	scope	slope

53

soap	tope	trope	antelope
antipope	bioscope	Good Hope	envelope
gyroscope	helioscope	heliotrope	horoscope
interlope	kaleidoscope	microscope	misanthrope
periscope	polyscope	stethoscope	telescope

OPSE, OPS

copse (And extend OP)

OPT

| Copt | adopt |
| | (And preterites of verbs in OP.) |

OR

for	lor	nor	or
Thor	tor	war	abhor
ambassador	ancestor	anterior	apparitor
auditor	bachelor	chancellor	competitor
compositor	conqueror	conspirator	contributor
corridor	councillor	counselor	creditor
cuspidor	editor	emperor	escritoire
excelsior	executor	expositor	exterior
furore	governor	inferior	inheritor
inquisitor	interior	junior	lessor
louis d'or	matador	memoir	metaphor
meteor	minotaur	mortgagor	orator
picador	posterior	progenitor	reservoir
rouge-et-et-noir	Salvador	seignior	senator
señor	servitor	solicitor	superior
vice-chancellor	warrior		

(Compare OAR.)

ORCE, ORSE, OARSE, OURCE

coarse	corse	course	force
gorse	hawse	hoarse	horse
morse	Norse	sauce	source
torse	concourse	discourse	divorce
endorse	enforce	perforce	recourse
remorse	resource	intercourse	unhorse

ORCH

| porch | scorch | torch | debauch |

ORD (as in "cord," see OARD) ORD (as in "word," see EARD)

ORGE

| forge | George | gorge | disgorge |
| engorge | regorge | overgorge | |

ORK

| cork | fork | pork | stork |
| torque | York | New York | |

(Compare ALK and AUK.)

ORLD (see EARLED)

ORM

form	norm	storm	swarm
warm	conform	chloroform	cruciform
cuneiform	deform	Great Orme	inform
iodoform	misinform	multiform	perform

54

| reform | transform | thunderstorm | uniform |
| vermiform | | | |

ORN, ORNE

born	borne	corn	horn
lorn	morn	scorn	shorn
sorn	sworn	thorn	torn
warn	worn	acorn	adorn
barley-corn	Cape Horn	Capricorn	forborne
forlorn	forsworn	Leghorn	lovelorn
peppercorn	suborn	unicorn	

(*Compare* OURN *and* AWN.)

ORP

| dorp | thorp | warp |

ORSE (see ORCE)
ORT

court	fort	forte	mort
ort	port	porte	quart
short	snort	sort	sport
swart	thwart	tort	wart
cavort	cohort	comport	consort
contort	deport	disport	distort
escort	exhort	export	extort
import	purport	rapport	report
resort	support	transport	misreport

(*Compare* AUT, AUGHT *and* OUGHT.)

ORTH

| forth | fourth | north | Porth |
| swarth | henceforth | thenceforth | |

OSE (*short*)

| dose | gross | jocose | morose |

OSE (*long*)

chose	close	clothes	does (*pl. of* "doe")
doze	froze	gloze	hose
nose	pose	prose	"pros"
rose	Rose	those	arose
banjos	compose	depose	depots
disclose	discompose	dispose	expose
foreclose	indispose	interpose	Montrose
redose	oppose	predispose	presuppose
recompose	repose	suppose	transpose
tuberose	unclose		

(For more than sixty other good rhymes, see plurals of
nouns and third person singulars of verbs in O, OW
and OE.)

OSH (*as in* "wash," *see* ASH)

OSS

boss	cross	doss	dross
floss	fosse	gloss	"Goss" (*china*)
joss	loss	moss	posse
Ross	toss	across	emboss
albatross	cerebos	reredos	

OST

| cost | frost | lost | wast |
| accost | exhaust | holocaust | pentecost |

(And preterites of OS, as in "bossed.")

OST *(as in "most," see OAST)*

OT, OTTE

blot	clot	cot	dot
got	grot	hot	jot
knot	lot	mot	not
plot	pot	rot	Scot
shot	slot	snot	sot
spot	squat	swat	swot
tot	trot	what	wot
yacht	Aldershot	aliquot	allot
apricot	bergamot	boycott	camelot
chariot	cocotte	compatriot	counterplot
echalot	forgot	gallipot	garotte
gavotte	idiot	patriot	polyglot
unbegot			

OTCH

blotch	botch	crotch	notch
potch	Scotch	watch	hop-scotch
hotch-potch			

OTE *(see OAT)*   OTH *(long, see OATH)*

OTH *(short)*

| broth | cloth | froth | Goth |
| moth | wroth | behemoth | |

OUCH

| couch | crouch | grouch | pouch |
| slouch | vouch | avouch | scaramouch |

OUCH *(soft)*

| mouch | debouch |

OUD, OWD

| cloud | crowd | dowd | loud |
| proud | shroud | Stroud | aloud |

(And preterites of OW, as in "bowed.")

OUGH *(see O, OCK, OFF, OW, UF)*   OUGHT *(see AUGHT)*

OUL *(see OAL)*   OULD *(see OLD)*

OUNCE

bounce	flounce	frounce	ounce
pounce	trounce	announce	denounce
pronounce	renounce		

OUND, OWNED

bound	found	ground	hound
mound	pound	round	sound
wound	abound	aground	around
astound	compound	confound	dumfound
expound	inbound	outbound	profound
propound	rebound	redound	resound
surround	unbound	unsound	underground

(And preterites and adjectives of words in OWN, as in "clowned" and "renowned.")

OUND (*as in "wound," an injury. See preterites of verbs in OON, as in "crooned"*)

OUNGE

lounge	scrounge

OUNT

count	fount	mount	account
amount	discount	dismount	miscount
paramount	recount	remount	surmount
tantamount			

OUP (*see OOP*)

OUR

dour	flour	hour	our
scour	sour	devour	

(Compare OWER in two-syllable rhymes.)

OURD

gourd	Lourdes	moored

(And extend OUR as in "toured.")

OURN

bourn	mourn

(Compare ORN.)

OURSE (*see ORCE*) OUS (*see US*)

OUS (*short*)

chouse	dowse	grouse	house
louse	mouse	nous	souse
carouse (*noun*)	charnel-house	custom-house	Strauss

OUSE (*long*)

drowse	blouse	blowze	browse
house (*verb*)	rouse	spouse	touse
carouse (*verb*)	espouse	unhouse	uprouse

(And plurals of nouns and third person singulars of verbs in OW and OUGH, as in "brows," "bows," "boughs" and "ploughs.")

OUT

bout	clout	doubt	drought
flout	gout	grout	knout

57

lout	nowt	out	owt
pout	rout	scout	shout
snout	spout	sprout	stout
tout	trout	about	devout
misdoubt	redoubt	roundabout	sauerkraut
throughout	waterspout	without	

OUTH

| drouth | Louth | mouth | south |

(For rhymes to "youth," see OOTH.)

OVE (*short*)

| dove | glove | love | shove |
| above | turtledove | | |

OVE (*long*)

clove	cove	drove	grove
hove	Hove	Jove	rove
stove	strove	throve	trove
wove	alcove	behove	interwove
treasure-troye			

(OVE, as in "proove," see OOVE.)

OW (*as in* "cow"), OUGH

bough	bow	brow	chow
cow	dhow	frau	how
now	plough	prow	row
scow	slough	Slough	sow
thou	trow	wow	vow
allow	avow	bow-wow	disallow
disendow	endow	enow	Foochow
kow-tow	somehow		

OW (*as in* "know," see O)

OWL, OUL

cowl	foul	fowl	ghoul (*also pronounced* "gool")
growl	jowl	owl	
prowl	scowl	befoul	

(Compare OWELL in two-syllable rhymes.)

OWN

brown	clown	crown	down
drown	frown	gown	noun
town	Cape Town	eiderdown	embrown
pronoun	renown	upside down	

OX, OCKS

box	"chocs."	cox	fox
ox	phlox	pox	approx.
equinox	heterodox	orthodox	paradox

(And plurals of nouns and third person singulars of verbs in OCK as in "frocks," "mocks.")

OY

boy	buoy	cloy	coy
gloy	hoy	joy	oi!
soy	toy	troy	Troy
alloy	Amoy	annoy	convoy
decoy	destroy	employ	enjoy
envoy	overjoy	pomeroy	Savoy

| saveloy | sepoy | | yoi-yoi! |

UB

blub	bub	chub	club
cub	drub	dub	grub
hub	pub	rub	scrub
shrub	snub	stub	sub
tub	hubbub	sillabub	Beelzebub

UBE

| cube | "rube" | tube | jujube |

UCE, USE

duce	juice	puce	use (*noun*)
abuse (*noun*)	conduce	deduce	diffuse
educe	excuse (*noun*)	introduce	obtuse
produce	reduce	refuse (*noun*)	seduce
traduce	abstruse		

(*Compare OOSE, hard, and, under same heading, UCE, without "u" sound, as in "truce."*)

UCH, UTCH

clutch	crutch	Dutch	hutch
much	such	touch	inasmuch
insomuch	overmuch	retouch	

UCK

buck	chuck	cluck	duck
luck	muck	pluck	puck
ruck	shuck	struck	suck
truck	tuck	thunderstruck	

UCT, UCKED

duct	abduct	aqueduct	conduct (*verb*)
deduct	induct	instruct	misconduct
obstruct	usufruct	viaduct	

(*And preterites of verbs in UCK, as in "mucked."*)

UD

blood	bud	cud	dud
flood	mud	rudd	scud
spud	stud	sud	thud

UDE (see OOD long)

UDGE

budge	drudge	fudge	grudge
judge	nudge	sludge	smudge
snudge	trudge	adjudge	misjudge
prejudge			

UE (see EW)

UFT

| cruft | tuft | | |

(*And past participles of verbs in UF.*)

UFF

bluff	buff	chough	chuff
clough	cuff	duff	fluff
Gough	gruff	guff	huff
luff	muff	puff	rough

59

U

ruff	scruff	slough	snuff
sough	stuff	tough	snuff
rebuff			enough

UISE (*see* OOSE *long*)   UIT (*see* OOT *long*)

UG

bug	chug	dug	drug
hug	jug	lug	mug
plug	pug	rug	shrug
slug	smug	snug	tug

UKE

| duke | fluke | Luke | puke |
| archduke | mameluke | peruke | rebuke |

UL, ULL (*as in* "bull")

bull	full	pull	wool
beautiful	bountiful	dutiful	fanciful
merciful	plentiful	powerful	sorrowful
wonderful	worshipful		

UL, ULL (*as in* "dull")

cull	dull	gull	hull
Hull	lull	mull	null
scull	skull	trull	annul
bulbul	disannul	numskull	seagull

ULE (*with* "u" *sounded*)

| mule | pule | tuhl | Yule |
| reticule | ridicule | vestibule | |

(*Compare* OOL, *and, under same heading,* ULE, *without
   "u" sound, as in* "rule." *Also* UEL *in two-syllable
   rhymes.*)

ULGE

| bulge | divulge | indulge | promulge |

ULK

| bulk | hulk | pulque | skulk |
| sulk | | | |

ULP

| gulp | pulp | sculp | |

ULSE

| mulse | pulse | appulse | convulse |
| expulse | impulse | insulse | repulse |

ULT

cult	ult	adult	catapult
consult	difficult	exult	insult
occult	result	tumult	

UM, BRUM

Brum	hum	chum	come
crumb	drum	dumb	glum
gum	hum	mum	mumm
numb	plum	plumb	rum
scrum	scum	slum	some
strum	sum	swum	thrum
thumb	become	benumb	

And false rhymes, as follows:

adventuresome	auditorium	burdensome	compendium
cranium	crematorium	cumbersome	delirium
effluvium	emporium	enconium	opithalamium
equilibrium	exordium	fee-fo-fum	frolicsome
gymnasium	harmonium	humdrum	humoursome
laudanum	magnesium	medium	mettlesome
millennium	minimum	misbecome	modicum
odium	opium	opprobium	palladium
pandemonium	pendulum	petroleum	premium
quarrelsome	residium	sanitorium	sensorium
solatium	spectrum	symposium	troublesome
tympanium	wearisome		

UME

fume	plume	spume	assume
consume	exhume	Fiume	illume
perfume	presume	relume	resume
reassume			

(*Compare* OOM.)

UMP

bump	chump	clump	dump
frump	grump	gump	hump
jump	lump	mump	plump
pump	rump	slump	stump
sump	thump	trump	

UN

bun	done	dun	fun
gun	Hun	none	nun
one	pun	run	shun
son	spun	stun	sun
ton	tun	won	anyone
begun	everyone	forerun	overdone
overrun	undone		

(*And about 100 false rhymes of words of three syllables and over ending in ON and TON, such as "criterion" and "skeleton."*)

UNCE

bunce	dunce	once

UNCH

brunch	bunch	crunch	hunch
lunch	munch	punch	scrunch

UNCT, UNKED

bunked	funked	adjunct	defunct
debunked			

UND

bund	fund	fecund	jocund
moribund	refund	rotund	rubicund
verecund			

(*And preterites of verbs in UN as in "punned."*)

UNE

dune	hewn	June	tune
viewn	commune	immune	importune

61

| impugn | inopportune | jejune | opportune |
| pursuen | subduen | triune | |

(Compare OON, and, under same heading, UNE with "u" not pronounced, as in "prune.")

UNG

bung	clung	dung	flung
hung	lung	rung	slung
sprung	strung	stung	sung
swung	tongue	wrung	young
among	Shantung	unhung	unsung

UNGE

| lunge | plunge | sponge | axunge |
| expunge | | | |

UNK

bunk	chunk	drunk	funk
hunk	junk	monk	plunk
punk	shrunk	skunk	slunk
spunk	stunk	sunk	trunk
quidnunc			

UNT

blunt	brunt	bunt	front
grunt	hunt	lunt	punt
runt	shunt	stunt	affront
confront			

UP

| crup | cup | pup | sup |
| tup | up | hiccough | |

UPE

| drupe | dupe | | |

(Compare OOP.)

UPT

| abrupt | corrupt | disrupt | |

(And preterites of verbs in UP, as in "cupped.")

UR *(see ER)*   URB *(see ERB)*   URD *(see EARD)*

URE

cure	dure	lure	Muir
pure	sure	abjure	adjure
conjure	cocksure	ensure	immure
insure	obscure	nomenclature	

(Compare OOR, also EWER in two-syllable rhymes.)

URF *(see ERF)*   URGE *(see ERGE)*

URK *(see ERK)*   URL *(see EARL)*

URN *(see EARN)*   URP *(see IRP)*

URSE *(see ERCE)*   URST *(see IRST)*

URT *(see ERT)*   URVE *(see ERVE)*

URZE

| furze | thyrse | | |

(And add "s" to words in ER, IR and UR.)

62

bus	buss	cuss	fuss
Gus	plus	pus	thus
truss	us	discuss	nonplus

(And nearly 300 false rhymes in words of three syllables and over, which end in US and OUS. Thus "sarcophagus" and "impetuous.")

USE (short, see UCE)
USE (long)

fuse	muse	use (*verb*)	abuse
accuse	amuse	confuse	contuse
diffuse	disabuse	disuse	enthuse
excuse	hypotenuse	peruse	Syracuse
transfuse			

(See EW, IFU, UE and OO for plurals of nouns and third person singulars of verbs, as in "pews," "adieus," "blues" and "moos." Compare OOSE and, under same heading, USE when "u" is not sounded, as in "peruse.")

USH (as in "bush")

bush	"cush"	push	ambush
	(*billiards*)		

USH (as in "blush")

blush	brush	crush	flush
frush	gush	hush	lush
mush	plush	rush	slush
thrush	tush		

USK

rusk	dusk	husk	musk
busk	tusk	Usk	

UST

bust	crust	dost	dust
gust	just	lust	must
rust	thrust	trust	adjust
august	disgust	distrust	entrust
incrust	mistrust	robust	unjust

(And preterites in USS, as in "fussed.")

UT, UTT

but	butt	crut	cut
glut	gut	hut	jut
Kut	mutt	nut	phut
putt	rut	scut	shut
slut	smut	strut	tut
abut	catgut	coconut	englut
gamut	halibut	occiput	rebut
waterbutt			

(For rhymes to "put," see OOT.)

UTE

Bute	"beaut"	chute	cute
jute	lute	mute	newt
suit	absolute	acute	arbute
argute	attribute	Canute	comminute
commute	compute	confute	constitute
contribute	depute	destitute	dilute

U

dispute	disrepute	dissolute	execute
impute	institute	irresolute	minute
parachute	persecute	pollute	prosecute
prostitute	pursuit	refute	repute
resolute	salute	substitute	transmute
volute			

(Compare OOT and, under same heading, UTE, when "u" is not sounded, as in "flute.")

UTH (see OOTH)

UX, UCKS

Bucks	crux	dux	flux
lux	conflux	efflux	influx
reflux			

(And plurals of nouns and third person singulars of verbs in UCK. Thus "ducks," "mucks.")

UZ

| buzz | coz | does | doz. |
| muzz | Uz | | |

Y

aye	buy	by	bye
cry	die	dry	dye
eye	fie	fly	fry
guy	Guy	hi!	hie
high	I	lie	lye
my	nigh	pie	ply
pry	rye	Rye	shy
sigh	sky	Skye	sly
spry	spy	sty	thigh
thy	tie	try	vie
why	wry	Wye	alkali
ally	amplify	apply	awry
beatify	beautify	belie	candefy
certify	clarify	classify	comply
crucify	decry	defy	deify
descry	dignify	disqualify	diversify
dignify	dulcify	edify	espy
falsify	fortify	Frenchify	fructify
glorify	go-by	good-bye	gratify
hereby	harmonify	horrify	imply
indemnify	intensify	justify	labefy
lenify	liquefy	lullaby	magnify
modify	mollify	mortify	multiply
notify	nullify	occupy	ossify
outcry	outfly	outvie	pacify
personify	petrify	preoccupy	prophecy
prophesy	purify	pūtrefy	qualify
ramify	rarefy	ratify	rectify
rely	reply	rubefy	sanctify
satisfy	scarify	Shanghai	signify
simplify	solidify	specify	stupefy
supply	tabefy	terrify	testify
thereby	typify	unify	untie
verify	versify	villify	whereby

(There are more than 2,000 words ending in Y short—thus "necessity." But these make very poor rhymes and are hardly worth consideration.)

YLE (*see* ILE)   YME (*see* IME)

YMPH

lymph   nymph

YNX (*see* INX)   YP (*see* IP)

YRE (*see* IRE)   YST (*see* IST)

YTH (*see* ITH)   YTHE (*see* ITHE)

YVE (*see* IVE)   YX (*see* IX)

END OF ONE-SYLLABLE SECTION

U

PART II

TWO SYLLABLE RHYMES

TWO-SYLLABLE RHYMES

ABARD

jabbered   scabbard   tabard

ABBER (*Extend AB for such words as "jabber," etc.*)

ABBLE

babble   dabble   drabble   gabble
rabble   scrabble   bedabble   bedrabble
(*For rhymes to "squabble," see* OBBLE.)

ABBOT

abbot   jabot   sabot

ABBEY, ABBY

abbey   flabby   shabby
(*And extend AB for such rhymes as "cabby."*)

ABEL (*see* ABLE)

ABID

rabid   tabid

ABIAN, ABION

fabian   gabion   Sabian   Arabian

ABIES

babies   gabies   Jabez   rabies
scabies

ABIT

habit   rabbit   cohabit   inhabit

ABLE, ABEL

Abel   able   babel   cable
fable   gabel   gable   label
Mabel   sable   stable   table
disable   enable   unable   unstable

ABOR, ABER

caber (*Scotch*) labor   neighbor   saber
tabor   belabor

ABY

baby   gaby   maybe

ACA

"bacca"   Dacca   paca   alpaca
malacca
(*Compare* ACKER.)

69

ACENT, ASCENT

jacent	nascent	adjacent	complacent
complaisant	interjacent	renascent	subjacent

ACET (see ASSET)

ACIAL

| glacial | racial | spatial | palatial |

ACID

| acid | flaccid | fracid | placid |

ACIOUS, ATIOUS

gracious	spacious	audacious	bibacious
bulbaceous	capacious	cetaceous	contumacious
cretaceous	disputatious	edacious	efficacious
fallacious	farinaceous	herbaceous	Horatius
Ignatius	incapacious	linguacious	loquacious
mendacious	minacious	mordacious	ostentatious
perspicacious	pertinacious	predaceous	procacious
pugnacious	rapacious	sagacious	salacious
saponaceous	sequacious	setaceous	tenacious
ungracious	veracious	vexatious	vivacious
voracious			

ACIS, ASIS

basis	glacis	oasis

(Compare plurals in ACE.)

ACKAGE

| package | trackage |

ACKEN

| blacken | bracken | slacken |

ACKER, ACQUER

| claquer | lacquer |

(And extend ACK for "blacker," etc.)

ACKET

bracket	jacket	packet	plaquet
racket			

ACKEY, ACKY

baccy	blackie	Jacky	lackey
quacky	tacky		

ACKLE (Extend AC and ACK for "cackle," "demoniacal," etc.)

ACTER, ACTOR (Extend ACK for "actor," "exacter," etc.)

ACTIC

| lactic | tactic | didactic | prophylactic |

ACTILE

| dactyle (or dactyl) | | tactile | tractile |

70

ACTION

action	faction	fraction	paction
taction	traction	abstraction	arefaction
attraction	benefaction	calefaction	co-action
compaction	contaction	contraction	counteraction
detraction	distraction	dissatisfaction	exaction
extraction	impaction	inaction	infaction
liquefaction	malefaction	petrifaction	protraction
putrefaction	rarefaction	reaction	refraction
retraction	retroaction	satisfaction	stupefaction
subaction	subtraction	transaction	

ACTIVE

active	tractive	abstractive	attractive
calefractive	distractive	inactive	petrifactive
protractive	purifactive	putrefactive	reactive
retractive	retroactive	stupefactive	

ACTRESS

actress	benefactress	detractress	malefactress

ACTURE

fracture	compacture	manufacture

ACY

Casey	Gracie	lacy	racy
Stracey			

ADAM

Adam	madam	macadam

ADDEN

bad'un	gladden	madden	sadden
Abaddon			

ADDER

adder	bladder	gadder	gladder
ladder	madder	padder	sadder

ADDEST, ADDIST

faddist	gladdest	maddest	saddest
sadist			

ADDLE

addle	faddle	paddle	raddle
saddle	spaddle	straddle	skedaddle

ADDOCK

Braddock	haddock	Maddock	paddock
shaddock			

ADDY

caddy	daddy	faddy	laddie
paddy			

ADEN, AIDEN

Aden	Haydn	laden	maiden
Sladen	overladen		

ADGER

badger	cadger

ADIENT

gradient	radiant

ADISH, ADDISH

baddish	caddish	gaddish.	radish

ADIUM

radium	stadium	palladium

ADLE

cradle	ladle

ADO

dado	spado	bastinado	bravado
crusado	desperado	Mikado	passado
tornado			

(Most of the above words may be pronounced with the "a" long or short.)

ADRE

cadre	padre

ADY, ADI

Brady	cadi	cady	lady
maidie	O'Brady	Sadie	shady

AFFER, AFFIR, AUGHER

chaffer	gaffer	Jaffa	Kaffir
laugher	quaffer	photographer	cinematographer

AFFIC

graphic	"maffick"	traffic	cinematographic
paragraphic	phonographic	photographic	pornographic
seismographic	seraphic	telegraphic	

AFFLE

baffle	raffle	snafile

AFFLED, AFFOLD

baffled	raffled	scaffold	snaffled

AFFY

café	chaffy	draffy	Taffy

AFTER

after	dafter	grafter	laughter
rafter	shafter	wafter	hereafter
thereinafter			

AGA, AGER (*hard*)

lager	saga

AGER, AJOR

gauger	major	(*And extend* AGE *for* "sager," *etc.*)

AGGARD

blackguard	haggard	laggard	staggered
swaggered			

AGGER

dagger	sagger	(*And extend* AG *for* "bragger," *etc.*)

AGGLE

draggle	gaggle	haggle	straggle
waggle	bedraggle		

AGGOT, AGATE

agate	Baggot	faggot	maggot

AGGY, AGGIE

Aggie	baggy	craggy	jaggy
knaggy	Maggie	quaggy	scraggy
shaggy	snaggy	swaggy	waggy

AGIC

magic	tragic	pelagic

AGILE

agile	fragile

AGO

dago	sago	Chicago	farrago
lumbago	Tobago	virago	

*(Most of the above words may be pronounced with either
the broad "a" or the narrow.) (Compare ARGO as in
"cargo," etc.)*

AGON

dragon	flagon	wagon

AGRANT

flagrant	fragrant	vagrant

AGSHIP

flagship	hagship

AIC

caique	algebraic	archaic	Hebraic
Judaic	mosaic	prosaic	

AIDEN (see ADEN)

AIETY, AITY

gaiety	laity

AILER

gaoler (*And extend* AIL *for "jailer," "sailor," etc.*)

AILIFF

bailiff	caliph

AILING

paling   grayling (*And extend* AIL *for "prevailing," etc.*)

AILMENT, ALMENT

(Extend AIL, ALE *for "ailment," "regalement," etc.)*

AILY, ALY

bailey	bailie	daily	Daly
gaily	greyly	maily	palely
scaly	shaly	snaily	stately
vale (*Latin*)			

AIMENT, AYMENT

claimant	clamant	payment	raiment
displayment	defrayment	repayment	

73

AINFUL, ANEFUL

baneful	gainful	painful	disdainful

AINTER
(Extend AINT for "quainter," etc.)

AINTLY

faintly	quaintly	saintly

AINY

brainy	drainy	grainy	rainy
Slaney	veiny	"champagney"	Delaney

AIRY, ARY

airy	chary	dairy	eyric
fairy	Gary	hairy	Mary
nary	prairie	snary	vary
wary	canary	Tipperary	vagary

(And many false rhymes, such as "ordinary," etc.)

AISER *(see AZOR)*   AISIN *(see AZEN)*   AISY *(see AZY)*

AITEN, ATAN

Dayton	Leyton	Satan	straighten
straiten			

AITER *(see ATER)*

AITHFUL

faithful	scatheful

AITRESS

creatress	traitress	waitress

AJOR *(see AGER)*

AKEN, ACON

bacon   *(And extend AKE for "awaken," etc.)*

AKER, ACRE

acher	acre	baker	fakir
nacre	Quaker	Straker	Long Acre
wiseacre			

(And extend AKE, AIK for "waker," "breaker" and other rhymes.)

AKO, ACCO

Jacko	shako	tobacco

AKY

achy	Blaikie	braky	flaky
quaky	shaky	snaky	

ALA

Bala	gala	Scala	cicala
	(Compare ARLER)		

ALACE, ALLOUS

callous	Dallas	palace	Pallas
phallus			
	(Compare ALICE)		

ALAD, ALLAD

ballad   salad

ALANCE

balance   valance

ALATE, ALLET, ALLOT

| ballot | mallet | palate | pallet |
| shallot | valet | | |

ALDER

alder   balder   Calder   scalder

ALDING

balding   scalding   Spalding

ALIA

| dahlia | failure | Thalia | Australia |
| interalia | regalia | Westphalia | |

ALIAN, ALIEN, ALION

alien	Thalian	Australian	bacchanalian
episcopalian	Pygmalion	tatterdemalion	sesquipedalian
Westphalian			

ALICE

Alice   chalice   malice   (*Compare* ALACE.)

ALID, ALLIED

| calid | dallied | pallid | rallied |
| sallied | tallied | valid | invalid (*adj.*) |

ALIPH (*see* AILIFF)

ALKER, AWKER, ORKER (extend ALK, AWK, ORK)

ALLANT

gallant   talent

ALLER, AWLER (extend ALL, AWL)   ALLET (*see* ALATE)
ALLIC

| Alec | Gallic | phallic | medallic |
| metallic | vandallic | | |

ALLION

| galleon | scallion | stallion | battalion |
| medallion | rapscallion | | |

ALLISH

| Dawlish | Gaulish | smallish | tallish |

ALLON

Alan   Allen   gallon   talon

ALLOP

| gallop | jalap | Salop | shallop |
| escallop | | | |

ALLOP (*broad*), OLLOP

dollop	gollop	scallop	wallop
trollop			

ALLOR

pallor	valour

ALLOW

aloe	callow	fallow	hallo
mallow	Mallow	sallow	shallow
tallow	(*Add "s" to the above for "gallows."*)		

ALLY

alley	ballet	bally	Calais
chalet	dally	galley	pally
rally	sally	Sally	tally
valley	reveille	shilly-shally	

(*A number of false rhymes by wrongly accentuating last two syllables of certain adverbs, such as "principally."*)

ALMER

calmer	palmer	embalmer	salaamer

(*Compare AMA and ARMER.*)

ALMEST, ALMIST

calmest	palmist	embalmist	psalmist

(*Compare ARMEST.*)

ALMON (*see AMMON*) ALMY (*see ARMY*)

ALTAR, ALTER, AULTER

altar	alter	falter	halter
Malta	palter	psalter	salter
vaulter	Walter	assaulter	defaulter
drysalter	Gibraltar		

ALTRY

paltry	psaltery	drysaltery

ALTY, AULTY

faulty	malty	salty	vaulty

AMA

Brahma	drama	lama	llama
Rama	Alabama	melodrama	pajama
Yokohama			

(*Compare ALMER and ARMER.*)

AMBEAU, AMBO

crambo	flambeau	Sambo	zambo

AMBER

amber	camber	clamber	tambour
timbre			

AMBIT

ambit	gambit

76

AMBLE

amble	bramble	Campbell	gamble
gambol	ramble	scamble	scramble
shamble	wamble	preamble	

AMBO (see AMBEAU)

AMEFUL

blameful	shameful

AMEL

camel	trammel	enamel

AMINE

famine	gamin	stamen	stamin
examine	cross-examine		

AMLET

camlet	hamlet	Hamlet	samlet

AMMAR, AMMER, AMOR

clamor	dammar	gammer	glamor
hammer	stammer	yammer	

(And extend AM for "crammer," &c.)

AMMON, ALMON

gammon	mammon	salmon	backgammon

AMMY

clammy	damme	drammie	gammy
hammy	jammy	mammy	Sammy
tammy	whammy		

AMPER

camper	champer	clamper	cramper
damper	hamper	pamper	ramper
scamper	stamper	tamper	tramper
vamper	decamper		

AMPLE

ample	sample	trample	example

AMPUS

campus	grampus	pampas	wampus

AMOUS, AMUS

amous	ramous	squamous	mandamus

ANA

lana	banana	bandana	Havana
iguana	Indiana	Juliana	Louisiana
Montana	Nirvana		

ANCER, ANSWER

answer	cancer	dancer	lancer
prancer	advancer	geomancer	necromancer
romancer			

ANCET, ANSIT

lancet	transit	Narragansett

ANCID

fancied	rancid

ANCHOR, ANCOUR (see ANKER)

ANCY

fancy	Nancy	aeromancy	arithomancy
cheiromancy	geomancy	hesitancy	lithomancy
necromancy	occupancy	onomancy	rhabdomancy
romancy	termagancy	vagrancy	

ANDAL (see ANDLE)

ANDAM, ANDEM, ANDOM

granddam	random	tandem	memorandum
nil desperandum			

ANDANT, ANDENT

candent	commandant	demandant

ANDATE, ANDIT

bandit	mandate	pandit

ANDA, ANDER, ANDOUR

blander	brander	candour	dander
gander	glander	grander	hander
panda	pander	slander	stander
Alexander	commander	coriander	demander
expander	gerrymander	Leander	Lysander
meander	oleander	philander	pomander
propaganda	reprimander	salamander	Uganda

ANDID, ANDED

candid

(And extend AND for "sanded," etc.)
(Compare ANDIED.)

ANDIED

bandied	brandied	candid	candied

ANDIER, ANDEUR

bandier	candier	grandeur	handier
sandier			

ANDISH

blandish	brandish	standish	outlandish

ANDIT (see ANDATE)

ANDLE, ANDAL

candle	dandle	Handel	handle
Randall	sandal	scandal	vandal
Coromandel			

ANDLER

chandler	dandler	handler	tallow-chandler

ANDOM (see ANDAM) ANDOUR (see ANDER)

ANDREL, ANDRIL

band-drill	hand-drill	mandrel	mandrill

ANDSOME (see ANSOM) ANDUM (see ANDAM)

ANDY

Andy	bandy	brandy	candy
dandy	Gandhi	handy	Kandy
randy	sandy	Sandy	shandy
organdie	unhandy		

ANEL, ANIL, ANNEL

anil	cannel	channel	flannel
panel	scrannel	empanel	

ANELY, AINLY (extend AIN, ANE) ANER, AINER (extend AIN, ANE)

ANET, ANNET, ANITE

gannet	granite	Janet	planet
Thanet	pomegranate		

ANGER (hard "g")

anger	banger	Bangor	clangor
ganger	hanger	languor	slanger
haranguer			

ANGER (soft "g")

changer	danger	manger	ranger
stranger	arranger	endanger	Grainger

ANGLE

angle	bangle	dangle	rangle
jangle	mangle	spangle	strangle
tangle	twangle	wangle	wrangle
disentangle	entangle	triangle	untangle

ANGLED, ANGLER, ANGLING (adapt above)

ANGO

mango	tango	contango	fandango

ANGUISH

anguish	languish

ANIC, ANNIC

Alnwick	panic	stannic	tannic
botanic	Britannic	diaphanic	galvanic
Germanic	mechanic	oceanic	organic
Romanic	Satanic	talismanic	titanic
tyrannic	volcanic		

ANIEL, ANNUAL

annual	Daniel	manual	spaniel
Nathaniel			

ANISH, ANNISH

banish	clannish	Danish	mannish
planish	Spanish	vanish	

ANATE (see ANET)
ANKARD, ANKERED, ANCHORED

anchored	bankered	cankered	hankered
tankard			

ANKER, ANCHOR, ANCOUR

anchor	Bianca	canker	rancor

(And extend ANK for "banker," etc.)

ANKLE		ANKLY (extend ANK)
ankle	rankle	

ANKY

Frankie	hankey	thankee	Yankee

(Extend ANK for "swanky," etc.)

ANLY

Cranleigh	Hanley	manly	Stanley

ANNA, ANNAH

anna	Anna	Hannah	manna
Havana	hosannah	Savannah	Susannah

(Compare ANA and ANNER.)

ANNER, ANOR

banner	canner	manner	manor
spanner	tanner		

(And extend AN for "fanner," etc.)

ANNEX

annex	panics	galvanics	mechanics

ANNON

cannon	Shannon	Clackmannan

ANON

| anon | canon | | |

ANNY

Annie	branny	canny	cranny
Fanny	granny	mannie	nanny
zany			

ANSACK

| Anzac | ransack | | |

ANSION

| mansion | scansion | stanchion | expansion |

ANSOM, ANDSOME

| handsome | hansom | ransom | transom |

ANSWER (see ANCER)

ANSY, ANTAM, ANTOM

| pansy | tansy | bantam | phantom |

ANTE, ANTI, ANTY

ante	anti	chanty	chianti
Dante	scanty	shanty	andante
Bacchante	dilettante		

ANTEL (see ANTLE)

ANTER

banter	canter	cantor	chanter
granter	grantor	panter	planter
ranter	scanter	decanter	descanter
displanter	enchanter	implanter	recanter
supplanter	transplanter	"Atlanta"	

ANTHER

| anther | panther | | |

ANTIC

| antic | frantic | Atlantic | corybantic |
| gigantic | pedantic | romantic | sycophantic |

ANTILE

| pantile | infantile | | |

ANTLE

| cantle | mantel | mantle | dismantle |

ANTLER

| antler | mantler | pantler | dismantler |

81

ANTLING

bantling   mantling   scantling   dismantling

ANTO, ANTEAU

canto   panto   esperanto   Lepanto
portmanteau

ANTOM (*see* ANTAM)   ANTY (*see* ANTE)

ANTRY

Bantry   chantry   gantry   pantry

ANNUAL (*see* ANIEL)   ANY (*see* ENNY)

ANYARD

lanyard   Spaniard   tan-yard

ANZA

stanza   bonanza   extravaganza   Sancho Panza
(*"Kansas" for plurals.*)

APAL (*see* APLE)   APEL (*see* APPLE)

APEN, APON

capon   misshapen   unshapen

APER, APIR, APOUR

caper   paper   tapir   vapour
(*Extend APE for "draper," etc.*)

APHIC (*see* AFFIC)

APID

rapid   sapid   vapid

APIST

papist   (*And extend APE for "shapest," etc.*)

APLE, APAL

maple   papal   staple   Naples (*for plurals*)

APLESS

capless   chapless   hapless   sapless
strapless   tapless   wrapless

APLING, APPLING

grappling   knappling   sapling

APNEL

grapnel   shrapnel

APOUR (*see* APER)   APPER (*extend* AP)

APPET

lappet   tappet

APPLE, APEL

| apple | chapel | dapple | grapple |
| knapple | scapple | scrapple | thrapple |

APPY

chappie   happy   (*And extend* **AP.**)

APTER, APTOR

apter   captor   chapter   adaptor

APTION

caption   adaption   collapsion   contraption

APTIST, APTEST

aptest   Baptist   adaptest   Anabaptist

APTURE

capture   rapture   enrapture

ARAB

Arab   scarab

ARBER, ARBOR

arbor   barber   harbor

ARBERED, ARBOARD

barbered   harbored   larboard   starboard

ARBLE, ARBEL

barbel   garble   marble

ARCEL

marcel   parcel   tarsal   tarsel
(*False rhymes in* "castle," "Newcastle," *etc.*)

ARCHER

archer   marcher   starcher   departure

ARCHY

Archy   starchy   Karachi

ARDEN, ARDON

garden   harden   pardon   Hawarden

ARDER

ardour   larder   "Nevada"   (*Extend* ARD.)

ARDY

hardy   lardy   mardy   tardy
Coolgardie   foolhardy

AREA, ARIER

area   charier   hairier   warier
Bavaria   Berengaria   Bulgaria   wistaria

AREL, ARREL, AROL

barrel   carol   Carroll   Darrell
apparel   (*"Harold" for past tense.*)

AREM, ARUM

Aram   harem   Sarum   alarum
harum-scarum

ARET, ARAT, ARRET, ARROT

arret   Barratt   carat   caret
carrot   claret   garret   parrot

ARGENT

argent   sergeant

ARGO, ARGOT

argot   cargo   Dargo   largo
Margot   embargo   supercargo   (*Compare* AGO.)

ARIAN, ARYAN

aryan   abecedarian   agrarian   Bavarian
barbarian   Bulgarian   centenarian   cessarian
disciplinarian   grammarian   librarian   predestinarian
proletarian   Rotarian   valetudinarian   vulgarian

ARIAT, ARIOT

chariot   Harriet   lariat   Marriott
Marryatt   Iscariot

ARIC

Garrick   barbaric   Pindaric

ARICE, ARRIS

Clarice	Harris	Paris

ARID, ARRIED

| arid | carried | harried | married |
| parried | tarried | miscarried | |

ARING, AIRING, EARING

charing   hair-ring
(*Extend ARE, AIR, EAR for "caring," "airing," "swearing," etc.*)

ARION, ARRION

carrion	clarion	Marion	Hilarion

ARIOUS

Darius	Marius	various	bifarious
contrarious	gregarious	nefarious	ovarious
precarious	vicarious	multifarious	temerarious

ARISH, EARISH

| bearish | fairish | garish | rarish |
| sparish | squarish | | |

ARITY

charity	clarity	parity	rarity
angularity	dissimilarity	irregularity	jocularity
particularity	perpendicularity	popularity	regularity
secularity	similarity	singularity	vulgarity

ARKEN

darken   hearken

ARKER

Osaka   (*Extend ARK for "barker," etc.*)

ARKET

market	parquet	Newmarket

ARKLE

| sparkle | hierarchal | matriarchal | monarchal |
| patriarchal | | | |

ARKLING

darkling   sparkling

ARKLY

darkly	sparkly	starkly

ARKY, AKI

barky	darkie	heark'ee	khaki
larky	marquee	parky	saki
sparky	Starkey	hierarchy	matriarchy

oligarchy   patriarchy

ARLER, ARLOUR

| marler | parlor | snarler | Transvaaler |

(Compare ALA.)

ARLET

| scarlet | starlit | varlet |

ARLEY, ARLY

| barley | Charlie | gnarly | Marley |
| parley | snarly | | |

(And extend AR for "particularly," etc.)

ARLIC

| garlic | Harlech |

ARLING

| darling | marling | snarling | sparling |
| starling | | | |

ARLOW

| Barlow | Carlow | Harlow | Marlow |

ARLY *(see ARLEY)*

ARMER, ARMOUR

| armor | Parma |

(And extend ARM for "charmer," etc.)

ARMEST, ALARMIST

alarmist

(And extend ARM for "harmest," etc. Compare ALMIST.)

ARMY, ALMY

| army | balmy | barmy | psalmy |
| smarmy | | | |

ARNAL, ARNEL

| carnal | charnel | darnel | Farnol |

ARNER

| darner | garner | yarner | *(Compare ANA.)* |

ARNET, ARNESS

| Barnet | garnet | incarnate | farness |
| harness | | | |

ARNEY

| barney | blarney | Carney | Killarney |
| ranee | | | |

ARNISH

garnish   tarnish   varnish

ARPER

carper   harper   scarper   sharper

ARRACK

arrack   barrack   carrack

ARRANT

arránt   apparent   transparent

ARRANT (*broad*), ORRENT

torrent   warrant   abhorrent

ARRAS

arras   Arras   harass   embarrass

ARREL (*see* AREL)   ARREL (*broad, as in "quarrel," see* ORAL)

ARREN, ARON

Arran   baron   barren   fanfaron
McLaren

ARREN (*broad*)

warren   foreign   sporran

ARRIAGE, ARAGE

carriage   Harwich   marriage   disparage
inter-marriage   miscarriage

ARRIER

barrier   carrier   farrier   harrier
marrier   parrier   tarrier

ARRIER (*broad*), ORRIOR

quarrier   sorrier   warrior

ARROW

arrow   barrow   Barrow   farrow
harrow   Harrow   Jarrow   marrow
narrow   sparrow   yarrow   Yarrow

ARRY

Barry   Carrie   carry   harry
Harry   Larry   marry   parry
tarry   miscarry   intermarry

ARRY (*long*)

sparry   starry   tarry (*from* "tar")

ARSHAL, ARTIAL

marshal   martial   partial   impartial

ARSLEY

parsley   sparsely

ARSON

arson   Carson   parson   squarson

ARTAN, ARTEN

Barton   carton   hearten   marten
smarten   Spartan   tartan   dishearten
kindergarten

ARTAR, ARTER

barter   carter   charter   darter
garter   martyr   parter   Satyr
smarter   starter   tartar   tarter
imparter   self-starter

ARTEL

cartel   startle

ARTFUL

artful   cartful   heartful

ARTIST, ARTEST

artist   chartist
   (*Extend* ART *for* "smartest," *etc.*)

ARTLET

martlet   partlet   tartlet   Bartlett

ARTNER

partner   heartener   smartener   disheartener

ARTRIDGE

cartridge   cart-ridge   partridge

ARTY

arty   hearty   parti   party
smarty   Astarte   Clancarty   ecarté

ARVEL

carvel   Darvel   marvel

ARVEST

carvest   harvest   starvest

ARY (see AIRY)

ASAL, AZEL

hazel   nasal

ASCAL, ASCHAL   ASCAR (see ASKER)

paschal   rascal

ASCENT

nascent   renascent   (And see ACENT)

ASCOT

Ascot   mascot

ASEMENT

basement	casement	abasement	debasement
defacement	displacement	effacement	emplacement
interlacement	misplacement	replacement	

ASHEN, ASHION, ASSION, ATION (short)

| ashen | fashion | passion | ration |
| compassion | dispassion | | |

ASHER

rasher   haberdasher

(And extend ASH for "masher," etc.)

ASHY

| ashy | flashy | mashie | sachet |
| splashy | trashy | | |

ASIA

| Asia | Dacia | fascia | acacia |
| Alsatia | Dalmatia | fantasia | |

ASIN, ASON, ASTEN

| basin | chasten | hasten | Jason |
| mason | | | |

ASIS (see ACIS)

ASKER, ASCA, ASCAR

| asker | basker | lascar | masker |
| tasker | Alaska | Madagascar | Nebraska |

ASKET

basket   casket   gasket

ASPER

asper	clasper	gasper	grasper
jasper	Jasper	rasper	

ASSEL

castle	tassel	vassal

ASSES

molasses (*And extend ASS for "asses," etc.*)

ASSET, ACET, ACIT

asset	basset	Brassett	facet
tacit			

ASSIC

classic	boracic	Jurassic	thoracic

ASSION (*see* ASHEN)
ASSIVE

massive	passive	impassive

ASSOCK

bassock	cassock	hassock

ASSY

brassie	brassy	chassis	classy
gassy	glacé	grassy	Jassy
lassie	massy	passé	Coomassie
Haile Selassie	Malagassy		

ASTARD, ASTERED

bastard	castored	dastard	mastered
plastered			

ASTEN (*see* ASIN)

ASTER (*short*)

aster	caster	castor	faster
master	pastor	plaster	vaster
alabaster	burgomaster	disaster	piastre
quartermaster			

ASTER (*long*)

baster	chaster	haster	paster
taster	waster	poetaster	

ASTIC

drastic	mastic	plastic	bombastic
ecclesiastic	elastic	enthusiastic	fantastic
gymnastic	Hudibrastic	iconoclastic	metaphrastic
monastic	periphrastic	pleonastic	sarcastic
scholastic			

90

ASTLY

ghastly	lastly	vastly

ASTY (as in "pasty.")

hasty	pasty	tasty

ASTY (as in "nasty.")

nasty	vasty

ATA (as in "data.")

data	strata	postulata	ultimata

ATA (as in "cantata.")

strata	cantata	errata	pro rata
sonata	(*Compare* AFTER.)		

ATAL

datal	fatal	natal

ATAN (see AITEN)

ATANT, ATENT

blatant	latent	natant	**patent**

ATCHET

Datchet	hatchet	latchet	**ratchet**

ATCHMAN

Scotchman	watchman

ATCHY

batchy	patchy	scratchy

ATER, ATOR

cater	crater	freighter	gaiter
greater	Hayter	mater	pater
straighter	traitor	waiter	alligator
commentator	cunctator	curator	equator
gladiator	scrutator	spectator	testator
valuator			

(*Extend* ATE *for about* 200 *other good rhymes. Thus*
"*hater*," "*navigator*," *etc.*)

ATHER (short)

blather	gather	lather	**rather**

ATHER (*long*)

farther father

ATHING (*see* AYTHING)

ATHOS

Athos bathos pathos

ATIAL (*see* ACIAL)

ATIC

attic	static	acrobatic	Adriatic
aerostatic	aquatic	aromatic	Asiatic
asthmatic	chromatic	climatic	dematic
dogmatic	dramatic	ecstatic	emblematic
emphatic	epigrammatic	erratic	fanatic
grammatic	Hanseatic	hydrostatic	idiomatic
mathematic	morganatic	muriatic	pancreatic
phlegmatic	pneumatic	pragmatic	prismatic
quadratic	rheumatic	schismatic	spermatic
stigmatic	symptomatic	systematic	traumatic

ATIN

Latin	matin	patin	satin
Prestatyn			

ATION, ATIAN

nation	ration	station	abbreviation
abdication	aberration	abjuration	ablation
abnegation	abomination	abrogation	accentuation
accumulation	accusation	actualization	adaptation
adjudication	administration	admiration	adoration
adulation	adulteration	adumbration	advocation
aeration	affectation	affidation	affirmation
afflation	agitation	aggravation	aggregation
agglomeration	alcoholization	alienation	alimentation
allegation	alleviation	alliteration	allocation
Alsatian	alteration	altercation	alternation
amalgamation	ambulation	amplification	amputation
anatomization	anhelation	animation	annexation
annihilation	annotation	annunciation	anticipation
appellation	application	approbation	appropriation
approximation	arbitration	argumentation	aromatization
arrogation	articulation	aspiration	assassination
assentation	asseveration	assignation	assimilation
association	attenuation	attestation	augmentation
auguration	auscultation	authorization	aviation
avocation	bifurcation	cachination	calcination
calculation	calumniation	cancellation	canonization
capitation	capitulation	captivation	carbonization
carnation	carnification	cassation	castigation
castration	causation	celebration	cementation
citation	civilization	clarification	classification
coagulation	cogitation	cognomination	cohabitation
collation	collimation	collocation	colonization
coloration	combination	commemoration	commendation
compensation	compilation	complication	compurgation
computation	concentration	conciliation	condemnation
condensation	condonation	confabulation	confederation

92

configuration	confirmation	confiscation	conflagration
conformation	confrontation	confutation	congelation
congratulation	congregation	conjugation	connotation
conservation	consideration	consolation	consolidation
contamination	contemplation	continuation	conversation
convocation	co-operation	co-ordination	copulation
coronation	correlation	corroboration	corrugation
coruscation	creation	cremation	crepitation
culmination	cultivation	cumulation	cunctation
curtation	curvation	dalmatian	damnation
debilitation	decimation	declamation	declaration
declination	decoration	decrustation	decussation
dedication	defalcation	defamation	defecation
defloration	degeneration	degradation	degustation
deification	delectation	delegation	delineation
dementation	demobilization	demonstration	denomination
denudation	denunciation	deodorization	depopulation
deportation	depreciation	depredation	deprivation
deputation	derivation	derogation	desecration
desiccation	designation	desolation	despoliation
destination	detestation	deterioration	determination
detonation	detruncation	devastation	deviation
dictation	differentiation	digitation	dignification
dilapidation	dilation	disapprobation	disclamation
disinclination	disintegration	dislocation	disobligation
disorganization	dispensation	disputation	dissemination
dissertation	dissimilation	dissipation	distillation
divagation	divarication	divination	domination
dotation	dubation	dulcification	duration
ebonification	economization	edentation	edification
education	edulcoration	effemination	ejaculation
elaboration	elation	electrification	elevation
elicitation	elimination	elongation	elutriation
emanation	emancipation	emasculation	embarkation
embrocation	emendation	emulation	enervation
enumeration	epuration	equalization	equation
equitation	equivocation	estimation	estivation
etiolation	evacuation	evagation	evagination
evangelization	evaporation	evocation	exacerbation
exaggeration	exaltation	examination	exasperation
excruciation	execration	exemplification	exhalation
exhilaration	exhortation	exhumation	exoneration
expiation	expiration	expiscation	explanation
explication	exploitation	exploration	exportation
expostulation	expurgation	extenuation	extermination
extirpation	extrication	exudation	exultation
exundation	fabrication	falcation	fascination
felicitation	fenestration	fermentation	ferrumination
fertilization	festination	figuration	filtration
fixation	flagellation	flagration	flammation
flirtation	florification	fluctuation	foliation
fomentation	formation	formication	fornication
fortification	fossilization	foundation	fructification
frumentation	frustration	fulmination	fumigation
furfuration	gelatination	gemnation	generalization
generation	germination	gestation	gesticulation
glaciation	glomeration	glorification	gravitation
gubernation	gustation	gyration	habitation
hallucination	hesitation	hibernation	hortation
humanization	humiliation	hypothecation	identification
illegitimization	illimitation	illiteration	illumination
illustration	imagination	immaculation	immanation

93

impersonation	imperturbation	implication	importation
imprecation	impregnation	impropriation	improvisation
imputation	inaffectation	inanimation	inapplication
inarticulation	inauguration	incantation	incapacitation
incarceration	incarnation	inceration	incineration
incitation	inclination	inconsideration	incorporation
incrimination	incrustation	incubation	inculcation
indication	indignation	indiscrimination	induration
inebriation	infatuation	infestation	infeudation
inflammation	inflation	information	ingemination
initiation	innervation	innovation	inoculation
inosculation	insanitation	insinuation	insolation
interpretation	interrogation	intimation	intonation
intoxication	inundation	investigation	invitation
invocation	irradiation	irrigation	irritation
isolation	iteration	jactitation	jaculation
jobation	jollification	jubilation	judaization
justification	laceration	lachrymation	lactation
lamentation	lapidation	lapidification	lauration
lavation	legation	legislation	legitimation
levigation	levitation	libation	libration
licentiation	ligation	limitation	lineation
liquation	liquidation	location	lubrication
lucubration	luctation	ludification	lunation
lustration	maceration	machination	mactation
manducation	manifestation	mastication	matriculation
mediation	medication	meditation	melioration
mellification	mensuration	migration	ministration
moderation	modification	modulation	molestation
mollification	moralization	mordication	mortification
multiplication	mutation	mutilation	mystification
narration	natation	nationalization	naturalization
nauseation	navigation	negation	negotiation
nictitation	nidification	nidulation	noctambulation
nodation	nomination	notation	notification
novation	nudation	nugation	nullification
numeration	nutation	obduration	obtestation
occulation	occupation	operation	oration
orbiculation	organization	origination	oscillation
oscultation	ossification	oxidation	oxygenation
pabulation	pacification	pagination	palliation
palpation	palpitation	panification	participation
pauperization	peculation	penetration	perambulation
percolation	perduration	peregrination	perforation
permeation	permutation	pernoctation	peroration
perscrutation	personation	personification	perspiration
perturbation	petrification	polarization	polliation
postillation	postulation	precipitation	predestination
predication	prefiguration	prejudication	prelation
premeditation	preoccupation	preparation	preponderation
preservation	prestidigitation	prevarication	prerelation
privation	probation	proclamation	procrastination
procreation	procuration	profanation	prognostication
prolation	prolification	prolongation	promulgation
pronunciation	propagation	propitiation	prorogation
provocation	publication	pulsation	punctuation
qualification	quotation	racemation	radiation
ramification	ratification	ratiocination	realization
recalcitration	recantation	recapitulation	reciprocation
recitation	reclamation	reclimation	recolonization
recreation	recrimination	rectification	recubation
redintegration	reduplication	re-examination	reformation
refrigeration	refutation	regeneration	registration
regulation	regurgitation	re-importation	reintegration

reiteration	rejuvenation	relation	relaxation
delegation	remonstration	remuneration	renovation
enunciation	reorganization	reparation	replication
representation	reprobation	repudiation	reservation
designation	respiration	restoration	resuscitation
retaliation	retardation	retraction	revelation
revivication	revocation	regation	reogation
rotation	ructation	rumination	salivation
salutation	salvation	sanctification	sanguification
satiation	saturation	scintillation	secularization
sensation	separation	sequestration	serration
siccation	signation	signification	simulation
situation	solicitation	solidification	sophistication
specialization	specification	speculation	spiritualization
spoliation	stabilization	stagnation	stellation
sternutation	stimulation	stipulation	stratification
stridulation	stultification	stylobation	subjugation
sublevation	subligation	sublimation	sublineation
subluxation	subordination	subornation	subrogation
succusation	sudation	suffocation	sulphuration
suppuration	suspiration	sustentation	syllabification
sartarization	taxation	temporization	temptation
testation	tergiversation	termination	testamentation
tentation	testification	thurification	titillation
turbation	toleration	tralation	tranquillization
transformation	translation	transmigration	transmutation
triangulation	tribulation	triplication	trepidation
truncation	turbination	ulceration	ululation
undervaluation	undulation	usurpation	vacation
vacillation	validation	valuation	vaporization
variegation	vaticination	vegetation	venation
venenation	veneration	ventilation	verbilization
vermiculation	vernation	versification	vesication
vexation	vibration	vigesimation	vilification
vindication	violation	visitation	vitiation
vitriolation	vituperation	vivification	vocalization
vocation	vociferation	volatilization	volcanization
vulcanization	vulneration		

ATIST (see ATTEST)
ATIVE, ATIFF

caitiff	dative	native	aggregative
creative	educative	operative	predicative
procreative	provocative		

ATLING, ATTLING

ratling	fatling	gatling	prattling
battling	spratling	tattling	tittle-tattling

ATO

Cato	Plato	potato	

ATOR (see ATER)

ATRAP

bat-trap	cat-trap	rat-trap	satrap

ATRIX

hat-tricks	matrix	administratrix	mediatrix
testatrix			

ATRON

matron	patron

ATTEN, ATON, ATEN

baton	batten	fatten	flatten
paten	patten	ratten	

ATTER

batter	blatter	chatter	clatter
fatter	flatter	hatter	latter
matter	patter	platter	scatter
shatter	smatter	spatter	tatter
bespatter			

ATTERN, ATURN

pattern	Saturn	slattern

ATTEST, ATIST, ATTICED

bratticed	fattest	latticed	statist

(And extend AT for "flattest," etc.)

ATTLE

battle	cattle	prattle	rattle
tattle	Seattle	tittle-tattle	

ATTLER, ATLER

tatler

(And extend ATTLE.)

ATTO, ATTEAU

chateau	gateau	plateau	mulatto

ATTY

batty	catty	chatty	fatty
gnatty	natty	Patti	patty
ratty	scatty	Cincinnati	

ATUM

datum	stratum	eratum	pomatum
postulatum	ultimatum		

ATURE *(long)*

nature	legislature	nomenclature

ATURE *(short)*, ATCHER

stature

(There is no good rhyme to this, but extensions of AC(and ATCH may be permitted, as in "catcher," "tacher," etc.)

ATUS

status   afflatus   apparatus   hiatus

ATY, EIGHTY, ATEY

eighty   Haiti   Katie   matey
slaty   weighty

AUCER

Chaucer   saucer   (*Compare* OARSER.)

AUCUS

raucus   Dorcas   raucous

AUCTION

ction   concoction   decoction

AUDAL

caudal   caudle   dawdle

AUDIT

audit   plaudit

AUDY, AWDY

bawdy   gaudy   Geordie   lordy
Maudie

AUFFEUR

chauffeur   gopher   loafer   sofa

AUGHTER (as in "laughter," see AFTER)
AUGHTER (as in "daughter")

daughter   slaughter   tauter   manslaughter
(*Compare* ORTER.)

AUGHTY

haughty   naughty   (*Compare* ORTY.)

AULIC

aulic   hydraulic   (*Compare* OLIC.)

AULTER (see ALTAR)

AULTY

ulty   malty   salty   vaulty

AUNDER

nder   maunder

AUNTER

| chaunter | gaunter | haunter | saunter |
| taunter | vaunter | | |

AUPER

| pauper | torpor | warper | |

AUSEOUS, AUTIOUS

| cautious | nauseous | | |

AUSER, AWSER

| causer | hawser | pauser | Mauser |

AUSTRAL

| austral | claustral | | |

AUTION

| caution | precaution | (*Compare* ORTION.) | |

AVA

| Ava | guava | Java | lava |
| larva | palaver | | |

(*Compare "carver" and other extensions of* ARVE.)

AVAGE

| lavage | ravage | savage | |

AVAL, AVEL

| naval | navel | save-all | Wavell |

AVEL (*short*)

| cavil | gavel | gravel | ravel |
| Savile | travel | unravel | |

AVELIN

| javelin | ravelin | | |

AVEMENT

| pavement | enslavement | | |

AVEN

| craven | graven | haven | raven |
| shaven | engraven | New Haven | |

AVER (*see* AVOUR)

AVERN, AVID

| cavern | tavern | avid | gravid |

AVIOUR

| pavior | saviour | wavier | Batavia |
| behavior | Belgravia | Moravia | |

AVIS

| avis | Davis | mavis | Mavis |

AVISH *(short)*

| lavish | ravish | McTavish |

AVISH *(long)*

| knavish | slavish |

AVOUR, AVER

| favor | flavor | savor | disfavor |
| semi-quaver | *(Extend AVE for "braver," etc.)* | | |

AVY

| cavy | Davy | gravy | navy |
| slavey | wavy | peccavi! | |

AVVY

| navvy | savvy |

AWDRY

| Audrey | bawdry | tawdry |

AWDY *(see AUDY)*   AWKER *(see ALKER)*

AWFUL

| awful | lawful |

AWKY, ALKY

| gawky | pawky | "talkie" | Milwaukee |

(Extend ALK for "stalky," etc. Compare ORKY.)

AWNING

awning

(Extend AWN and ORN for "dawning," "morning," etc.)

AWNY

brawny	fawny	Pawnee	sawney
scrawny	Shawnee	tawny	yawny
mulligatawny	*(Compare ORNY.)*		

99

AWYER

lawyer   sawyer

AXEN, AXON

flaxen   Jackson   Saxon   waxen

AXY

flaxy   Laxey   taxi   waxy
ataxy

AYDAY, EYDAY

heyday   payday   playday   May Day

AYER, EYOR
(*Extend* AY *and* EY *for* "gayer," "surveyor," *etc.*)

AYMAN

cayman   Damon   drayman   flamen
hay-man   layman   Ramon   highwayman

AYTHING

bathing   plaything   scathing swathing

AZA

Gaza   plaza   Zaza

AZARD

brassard   hazard   mazard

AZEL (*see* ASAL)

AZEN, AZON, AISIN

blazon   brazen   raisin   diapason
emblazon

AZOR, AISER

praiser   Fraser   razor
(*And extend* AISE *and* AZE.)

AZIER

brazier   crazier   glazier   hazier
lazier

AZY, AISY

crazy   daisy   Daisy   hazy
lazy   mazy   Maisie   quasi

AZZLE

Basil	dazzle	drazil	frazzle
razzle	bedazzle	frazzle-dazzle	

EA

idea	Korea	Judea	panacea
ratifia			

EACHER, EATURE, EECHER

creature	feature	(And extend EACH and EECH)

EACHY (extend EACH)

EACON

beacon	deacon	weaken

EADEN (short)

deaden	Heddon	leaden	redden
Sedden	threaden		

EADER, EDAR, EDER, EEDER

cedar	(And extend EAD, EDE and EED.)

EADLE, EEDLE

beadle	Cheadle	daedal	needle
predal	tweedle	wheedle	bipedal

EADLOCK

deadlock	wedlock

EADWAY

dead-way	headway	Medway

EADY (short, see EDDY)   EADY (long, see EEDY)
EAFER

deafer	heifer	zephyr	Strathpeffer
"whateffer"			

EAFEST

deafest	prefaced

EAFY, EEFY

beefy	feoffee	Fifi	leafy
reefy	sheafy		

EAGER, EAGRE, EAGUER, IGUER

eager	leaguer	meagre	beleaguer
intriguer			

EAGLE, EGAL

beagle	eagle	gregal	legal
regal	sea-gull	illegal	inveigle

EAKEN (see EACON)

EAKER, EEKER

beaker   speaker   *(And extend EAK, EEK.)*

EAKING

sea-king
(And extend EAK and EEK for "speaking," "seeking," etc.)

EAKLING

meekling   treacling   weakling

EAKY, EEKY

beaky   cheeky   cliquey
(And extend EAK.)

EAL

real   ideal   unreal   hymeneal
(Compare EAL and EEL in one-syllable rhymes.)

EALER, EELER, EALING *(extend EAL and EEL in one-syllable rhymes.)*

EALOT (see ELATE)

EALOUS

jealous   zealous   Marcellus

EALTHY

healthy   stealthy   wealthy

EALTY

fealty   realty

EALY

Ely   freely   Healy   mealy
squealy   steely   genteely   Matabele
ukulele

EAMAN, EEMAN, EMAN, EMON

beeman   demon   freeman   gleeman
he-man   leman   seaman   semen
tea-man

EAMER, EMER, EMUR

Braemar   emir   femur   lemur
(And extend words under EAM for "dreamer," "schemer," etc.)

EAMISH

beamish   dreamish   squeamish

EAMSTER (see EEMSTER)

EAMY

creamy	dreamy	seamy	streamy

EAN, IEN, IAN

Ian	lien	pæan	Korean
empyrean	epicurean	European	Fijian
Hawaiian	herculean	hymenean	Jacobean
Judean	plebian	pygmean	Pythagorean

EANER, EANOUR

demeanour

> (*And extend words under EAN for "greener," "cleaner," "obscener," etc.*)

EANEST, EENIST, ENIST

plenist   machinist

> (*Extend words under EAN in one-syllable rhymes for "cleanest," "obscenist," etc.*)

EANING, EANLY, EENLY, ENELY, EAPER, EEPER, EEPY (see one-syllable rhymes and extend)

EANO

beano	Reno	Albino	bambino
casino	maraschino	merino	Filipino

EARANCE, ERENCE, EARER, EARCHER, IRCHER, URCHER (see EAR, EARCH, IRCH, etc., and extend.)

EAREST, ERIST

merest	querist	theorist

> (*And extend EAR, EER and ERE.*)

EARETH, ERITH

Erith   (*Extend EAR for "heareth," etc.*)

EARFUL

cheerful	earful	fearful	tearful

EARIER, EERIER, ERIOR

eerier	anterior	inferior	interior
Liberia	posterior	Siberia	superior

> (*And extend EARY, EERY for "wearier," "beerier," etc.*)

EARING, EERING

earring

> (*And extend EAR, EER for "hearing," "leering," etc.*)

EARLY, IRLY, URLY

burly	curly	early	girlie
pearly	Purley	Shirley	twirly

103

EARLY, EERLY, ERELY
(*Extend* EAR, EER, ERE *for "clearly," "merely," etc.*)

EARMENT
cerement   endearment

EARNER, IRNER, URNER, EARNING, IRNING, URNING (*extend words under* EARN)

EARNESS, EERNESS
sheerness
(*And extend* EAR *and* EER *for "clearness," "queerness," etc.*)

EARNEST, ERNEST, URNEST
earnest   Ernest   furnaced
(*And extend words under* EARN *for "sternest," "burnest," etc.*)

EARY, EERY, ERY
Erie	eerie	dearie	Leary
peri	query	Dundreary	theory

(*And extend* EAR *and* EER *for "weary," "beery," etc.*)

EASAND
reasoned   seasoned   treasoned   weasand

EASANT, ESCENT
crescent	peasant	pheasant	pleasant
present	convalescent	decrescent	deliquescent
delitescent	effervescent	efflorescent	excrescent
incessant	obsolescent	phosphorescent	putrescent
quiescent			

EASAR, EASER
Cæsar	geezer	geyser	sizar
Ebenezer			

(*And extend certain words under* EASE.)

EASEL
Diesel   easel   measle   weasel

EASON
reason   season   treason

EASTER
Easter   northeaster   (*And extend* EAST.)

EASTING
bee-sting   feasting

EASTLY

beastly	priestly

EASURE, EISURE

leisure	measure	pleasure	treasure
displeasure			

EASY, EEZY

breezy	cheesy	easy	freezy
greasy	queasy	sleazy	sneezy
wheezy	Brindisi		

EATEN, EETEN

Beeton	Cretan	Eton	seton

(And extend EAT and EET for "beaten," "sweeten," etc.)

EATER, EETER, ETA, ETER, ETRE

beta	Greta	litre	meter
Peter	prætor	goldbeater	saltpeter
two-seater			

(Extend EAT and EET.)

EATHER (short), ETHER

blether	feather	heather	Heather
leather	nether	tether	weather
wether	whether	altogether	together

EATHER (long)

breather	either	neither	seether

EATHING, EETHING

breathing	seething	tea-thing	teething
wreathing	bequeathing		

EATURE

creature	feature	*(Compare EACHER.)*

EATY, EETY

Beattie	meaty	peaty	sleety
sweetie	Otaheiti	Tahiti	

EAVEN, EVEN

Bevan	Devon	Evan	Heaven
leaven	Leven	seven	eleven

EAVER

beaver	Belvoir	Eva	fever
leaver	lever	stiver	viva
Geneva	Siva		

(And extend rhymes under EAVE; thus "cleaver," "deceiver," etc.)

EAVY EVY

bevy	chevvy	heavy	levy
levée	"nevvy"		

EBE

Bebe	Hebe	Phœbe

EBEL, EBBLE

pebble	rebel	treble

EEBLE

feeble	Keble

ECCA

Mecca	Rebecca	(*Compare* ECKER.)

ECENT

decent	puissant	recent	indecent

ECHER, ETCHER

etcher	fetcher	fletcher	lecher
retcher	sketcher	stretcher	

ECHO

echo	gecko	secco	"dekko"

ECIAN, ETION

Grecian	accretion	completion	depletion
deletion	excretion	Phœnician	repletion
secretion	Venetian		

ECIES

Decies	nieces	species	thesis

(*Add "s" to certain words under* EACE; *thus "fleeces,"
"ceases," "mantelpieces," etc.*)

ECIOUS

specious	facetious

ECKER, EQUER

"brekker"	Flecker	exchequer

(*And extend* ECK *and* EQUE. *Compare* ECCA.)

ECKLE, EKEL

treckle	heckle	keckle	shekel
speckle	("Beccles" *and* "Eccles" *for plurals.*)		

ECKLESS, ECKLACE

feckless	checkless	necklace	reckless
speckless			

ECKON

beckon reckon

(Preterites of same to rhyme with "second" and "fecund.")

ECTIC

hectic   eclectic   electric

ECTION, EXION and ECTIVE

flection   vection   complexion   invective
(And extend ECT and EX for "section," "connection," "detective," "subjective," etc.)

ECTOR, ECTRE

hector   Hector   nectar   rector
specter   vector   *(And extend ECT.)*

ECTURE

lecture   architecture   conjecture   prefecture

EDAL, EDDLE, EDULE

medal   meddle   pedal   peddle
reddle   schedule   treadle   intermeddle

EDAR

cedar   *(And extend EAD for "pleader," etc.)*

EDDY, EADY

eddy   Freddy   heady   Neddy
ready   shreddy   steady   Teddy
already

EDEN

Eden   Sweden

EDENCE

credence   antecedence   precedence

EDENT

credent   needn't   sedent   antecedent

EDGER

edger   dredger   hedger   ledger
pledger   sledger   wedger

EDGWARE

Edgware   sledge-wear

107

EDIT

edit · · · credit · · · discredit · · · sub-edit

EDIUM

medium · · · tedium

EDLAR

medlar · · · meddler · · · pedlar · · · peddler
scheduler

EEDLESS, EEDLY (extend EAD and EED)

EDLEY, EADLY

deadly · · · medley · · · redly · · · Sedley

EDO

credò · · · Toledo · · · torpedo · · · lido
libido

EECHY, EACHY (extend EACH, EECH)

EECY

fleecy · · · greasy

EEDLESS, EEDY, EADY (extend EAD and EED)

EEMSTER

deemster · · · teamster

EENISH, EANISH (extend EAN and EEN in one-syllable rhymes.)

EENY, ENE

greeny · · · "tweenie" · · · Athene · · · nota-bene
Proserpine · · · Queenie

EEPIER

creepier · · · sleepier · · · leap-year

EEPLE, EOPLE

people · · · steeple

EERAGE

beerage · · · clearage · · · peerage · · · steerage

EESTONE

freestone · · · keystone · · · sea-stone

EETLE

beetle betel decretal

EEVISH, IEVISH

peevish thievish

EEZER (*see* EASAR)

EFTY

hefty lefty wefty

EGAL (*see* EAGLE)

EGGAR, EGGER

beggar dregger egger kegger
pegger

EGGY

dreggy eggy leggy Meggie
Peggy

EGIAN, EGION

Fijian legion region collegian
Glaswegian Norwegian

EGNANT

pregnant regnant

EGRESS

egress negress regress

EGRET

egret regret

EIFER (*see* EAFER)

EIGHBOR *and* EIGHTY (*see* ABOR *and* ATY)
EIRESS

heiress mayoress

EIST

deist beest fleest freest
seest

EITHER ("e" sounded)

ether (*And see* EATHER.)

EITHER ("i" sounded)

blither either lither mither
neither scyther tither writher

ELATE, ELOT

helot prelate stellate zealot

109

appellate   constellate

ELDAM, ELDOM
beldam   seldom

ELDER, ELDEST, ELDING (*extend* ELD)

ELFISH
elfish   selfish   shell-fish

ELIC
relic   telic   angelic

ELINE
bee-line   feline   sea-line

ELISH, ELLISH
hellish   relish   embellish

ELLA
Bella   Ella   Stella   Arabella
prunella   umbrella   (*Compare* Eller.)

ELLER (*extend* ELL)

ELLIST, ELLISED
trellised   'cellist   (*And extend* ELL *for* "dwellest," *etc.*)

'ELLO, ELLOF, ELLOW
bellow   'cello   fellow   mellow
yellow   duello   Martello   Portobello
prunello   Punchinello   violoncello

ELLY
belly   jelly   Kelly   Nelly
Shelley   smelly

ELON
felon   melon

ELPER
Belper   helper   yelper

ELSIE
Elsie   Chelsea   Selsey

ELTA, ELTER
delta   helter   shelter   skelter
smelter   svelter   swelter   welter
(*And extend* ELT.)

EMBER
ember   member   December   dismember
November   remember   September

EMBLE

Kemble	tremble	assemble	dissemble
resemble			

EMBLY

trembly	Wembley	assembly

EMI, EMMY

clemmy	demi	hemi	Jemmy
semi			

EMIER, EAMIER

creamier	dreamier	premier	steamier

EMISES

nemesis	premises

EMISH

blemish	Flemish	phlegmish

EMIST

chemist	hemmest	premised	stemmest

ÉMLIN

Kremlin	gremlin	Fremlin

EMOR

hemmer	tremor	condemner

EMPLAR

templar	exemplar

EMPTION

emption	ademption	co-emption
pre-emption	redemption	

EMU   EMUR (see EAMER)

emu	seamew

EMUSE

bemuse	emus	seamews

ENA

Ena	Lena	Nina	scena
Tina	Zena	arena	concertina
hyena	lena	Modena	ocarina
patina	Pasadena	semolina	signorina
Tsarina			

(*And compare* EANER *and* EANOUR.)

ENACE, ENNIS, ENNOUS

Dennis	menace	pennous	tenace
tennis	Venice	impennous	vaginopennous

111

ENAL

penal   renal   venal   duodenal

ENANT

pennant   tenant   lieutenant

ENATE (see ENNET)

ENSA, ENCER

censer   censor   spencer
(And extend ENCE and ENSE for "fencer," "denser," etc.)

ENCEFORTH

henceforth   thenceforth

ENCHER, ENSURE, ENTURE

censure   venture   adventure   debenture
indenture   misadventure   peradventure
(And extend ENCH for "bencher," "quencher," etc.)

ENCIL, ENSAL

mensal   pencil   stencil   prehensile
utensil

ENDANT, ENDENT

pendant   pendent   splendent   attendant
resplendent
(And extend END for "defendant," etc.)

ENDER, ENDOR, ENDA

Brenda   fender   gender   slender
splendor   Zenda   surrender
(And extend END for "lender," "defender," etc.)

ENDON

Hendon   tendon

ENGLISH

English   jinglish   tinglish

ENGTHEN

lengthen   strengthen

ENIAL

genial   menial   venial   congenial

ENIC

scenic   splenic   arsenic *(adj.)*   eugenic
photogenic   *(Pluralize "scenic" to rhyme with "Phoenix.")*

ENIN

Benin   Lenin   Menin

ENIOR

senior   señor   signor   teenier
weenier

ENISH

rhenish   tenish   replenish

ENIST (see EANEST)

ENNA

henna   senna   duenna   Gehenna
sienna   Vienna

ENNEL

fennel   kennel   phenyl

ENNER, ENOR, ENOUR

tenor   tenour   (And extend EN.)

ENITH, ENNETH

Kenneth   zenith

ENNET, ENATE

Bennett   jennet   kennet   rennet
senato   tenet

ENNIS (see ENACE)

ENNON, ENON

pennon   tenon

ENNY, ANY

any   Benny   Denny   fenny
Jenny   many   penny   wenny
Abergavenny   Kilkenny

ENSER (see ENCER)   ENSILE (see ENCIL)

ENSIVE

pensive   (And extend ENCE and ENSE for "expensive," etc.)

ENSION (see ENTIAN)

ENTAIL

entail   ventail

ENTAL, ENTIL, ENTLE

dental   gentle   lentil   mental
rental   trental
(And extend ENT for "accidental," "ornamental," etc.)

ENTANCE, ENTENCE

sentence   repentance

ENTER, ENTOR

centaur	center	enter	mentor

(And extend ENT for "renter," "tormentor," etc.)

ENTIAN, ENTION, ENSIAN

gentian	mention	pension	tension
abstention	accension	ascension	convention
detention	dimension	dissension	intension
intention	intervention	supervention	

(And extend END and ENT for "distension," "attention," etc.)

ENTICE, ENTIS

pentice	prentice	apprentice	compos mentis

ENTILE

Gentile	pentile

ENTIST, ENTEST, ENTICED

dentist	prenticed	apprenticed

(And extend ENT for "scentest," etc.)

ENTLE, ENTIL (*see* ENTAL)

ENTRAL

central	ventral

ENTRY

entry	gentry	sentry	comment'ry
element'ry	invent'ry	parliament'ry	

ENTURE

denture	venture	adventure	debenture
indenture	misadventure	peradventure	

(And compare ENCHER.)

ENTY

plenty	scenty	twenty	dolce far niente
festina lente			

ENU

menu	venue

ENUS

genus	Venus

EO

Cleo	Leo	Rio	trio
yeo			

EOLE

creole	key-hole

EON

æon	Ian	Leon	neon
peon	Fijian	Hawaiian	plebeian

114

EOPARD, EPHERD, EPPERED

leopard   peppered   shepherd

EPID

tepid   trepid   intrepid

EPOT

Beppo   depot   Aleppo

EPPER, EPER

leper   pepper   stepper

EPPING

Epping   stepping

EPPY

peppy   Sheppey

EPTIC

peptic   sceptic   septic   antiseptic
dyspeptic   enpeptic   epileptic

EPTOR

sceptre   acceptor   preceptor   interceptor

EQUAL, EQUEL

equal   sequel   co-equal   unequal

EQUENCE

frequence   sequence

ERA

era   lira   Vera   chimera
(Compare EARER, for which extend EAR.)

ERALD

Gerald   ferruled   herald   imperilled

ERBAL, URBLE

burble   herbal   verbal

ERCER, ERSER, URSAR

bursar   curser   mercer   nurser
purser   *(And extend ERSE for "terser," etc.)*

ERCY, URSY

Circe   mercy   nursey   Percy
pursy   controversy   grammercy

EREAL, ERIAL

cereal	ferial	serial	arterial
ethereal	funereal	immaterial	imperial
material	ministerial	venereal	

ERGER, ERDURE, URGER

burgher	merger	perjure	purger
scourger	urger	verdure	verger
deterger			

ERET (*see* ERIT)

ERGY, IRGY, URGY

clergy	dirgy	sergy	surgy

ERIC, ERRICK

Berwick	cleric	Derek	derrick
Eric	ferric	Herrick	Lerwick
spheric	atmospheric	enteric	generic
hemispheric	Homeric	hysteric	numeric

ERIL, ERRULE, ERYL

beryl	Beryl	Errol	ferrule
Merrall	peril	spherule	

ERISH

cherish	perish

ERIT, ERRET

ferret	merit	disinherit
inherit	demerit	

ERJURE (*see* ERGER)

ERKIN

firkin	gherkin	jerkin	merkin
Perkin			

ERKY, URKY

jerky	murky	perky	smirky
turkey	Turkey		

ERLING (*see* IRLING)

ERMAN, ERMON

Burman	Firman	German	Herman
merman	sermon	Omdurman	

ERMENT

ferment	averment	bestirment	determent
interment	preferment		

ERMIN, ERMINE

ermine	vermin	determine	predetermine

116

ERMIT

hermit	Kermit	permit (*noun*)	"termit"

ERNAL, ERNEL, OLONEL, OURNAL, URNAL

colonel	journal	kernel	sternal
vernal	diurnal	eternal	external
hodiernal	infernal	internal	fraternal
maternal	nocturnal	paternal	sempiternal
supernal			

ERNARD

Bernard	gurnard

ERO

hero	Nero	pierrot	zero
bandolero	bolero	montero	sombrero

ERRAND

errand	gerund

ERRIER

burier	ferrier	merrier	terrier

ERING

derring	herring

ERY (*as in* "query," *see* EARY)   ERRULE (*see* ERIL)

ERRY

berry	bury	Bury	cherry
Derry	ferry	jerry	Kerry
merry	perry	sherry	skerry
very	wherry	Londonderry	Pondicherry

ERSEY, URZY

furzy	jersey	Jersey	kersey
Mersey	New Jersey		

ERSIAN, ERSION, ERTIAN, URSION

mersion	Persian	tertian	version
abstention	animadversion	aspersion	assertion
aversion	coercion	conversion	demersion
desertion	detersion	dispersion	diversion
emersion	excursion	exertion	immersion
incursion	insertion	inversion	perversion
reversion	subversion		

ERSON, ORSEN

person	urson	worsen	McPherson

ERSUS

thyrsus	versus

ERTAIN, URTAIN

Burton	certain	curtain	Girton
Merton	uncertain		

117

ERTER, IRTER, URTER, ERTEST, ERTLY, URTLY
(extend ERT, IRT and URT)

ERVANT, ERVENT
fervent   servant   observant

ERVER, ERVOR
fervor   (And extend ERVE for "server," etc.)

ERVID
fervid   scurvied   perfervid
(And accentuate final syllables of certain words in ERVE and URVE. Thus "curved," etc.)

ERVISH
curvish   dervish   nervish   swervish

ERVY, URVY
curvy   nervy   scurvy   topsy-turvy

ESAGE, ESSAGE
message   presage

ESCENCE, ESSENCE
essence	adolescence	coalescence	convalescence
delitescence	effervescence	efflorescence	excrescence
obsolescence	phosphorescence	pubescence	putrescence
quiescence	quintessence	senescence	turgescence

ESCIENCE
nescience   prescience

ESCO
fresco   Tresco   alfresco

ESCU
fescue   rescue

ESENCE, EASANCE
pleasance   presence   omnipresence

ESION
lesion	adhesion	cohesion	Ephesian
inhesion	magnesion	Polynesian	

ESIS
species   thesis   aposiopesis   exegesis
(And extend certain words under EACE for "ceases," etc.)

ESSAGE (see ESAGE)

ESSENCE (see ESCENCE)   ESSEL (see ESTLE)

ESSER, ESSOR

dresser   lesser   lessor   messer
presser   (*And extend ESS for "transgressor," etc.*)

ESION

session   concession   discretion   secession
    (*And extend ESS for "profession," etc.*)

ESSURE

pressure   (*And extend ESH for "flesher," "refresher," etc.*)

ESSY

Bessie   Crecy   dressy   essay
Jessie   messy   Tessie

ESTAL, ESTLE

festal   pestle   vestal

ESTER

Chester   Esther   fester   Hester
jester   Leicester   sou'wester
    (*And extend EST for "tester," "molester," etc.*)

ESTIAL

bestial   celestial

ESTIGE

prestige   vestige

ESTINE

destine   mess-tin   clandestine   intestine
predestine

ESTIVE

estive   festive   restive   digestive
investive   suggestive

ESTLE (*silent "t"*)

Cecil   nestle   trestle   vessel
wrestle   (*Extend above for rhymes to ESTLER.*)

ESTO

presto   manifesto

ESTRAL, ESTREL

kestrel   ancestral   orchestral

ESTURE

gesture   vesture   divesture

119

ESTY

| chesty | resty | testy | yesty |

ETCHER (*see* ECHER)

ETHEL

| Bethel | Ethel | methyl |

ETFUL (extend ET for "fretful," "forgetful," etc.)

ETHER (*see* EATHER)   ETOR, ETER
(*see* EATER)

ETTER, ETTOR

fetter   (*And extend ET for "better," "debtor," etc.*)

ETTISH, ETISH

fetish   Lettish   (*And extend ET for "pettish," etc.*)

ETTLE, ETAL

| fettle | kettle | metal | mettle |
| nettle | petal | settle | unsettle |

ETTO

| ghetto | petto | falsetto | lazaretto |
| libretto | stiletto | | |

ETTY, ETI, ETTI

Betty	fretty	Hetty	jetty
Letty	petty	sweaty	confetti
spaghetti	spermaceti		

EUDAL (*see* OODLE)   EUTER (*see* OOTER)

EVEL

| bevel | devil | Greville | level |
| Neville | revel | dishevel | |

EVER (short)

clever	ever	never	sever
Trevor	assever	dissever	endeavour
however	whatever	whenever	wherever
whoever	(*For EVER, as in "fever," see EAVER.*)		

EVEREST

| Everest | cleverest | severest |

EVIL

| evil | weevil | coeval | primeval |
| medieval | | | |

EVIOUS

| devious | previous |

EVY (*see* EAVY)

EWAGE

| brewage | "New Age" | sewage | escuage |

EWARD, EWERED

| leeward | Seward | steward | sewered |
| skewered | | | |

EWEL, UEL

crewel	cruel	dual	duel
Ewell	fuel	gruel	jewel
ruelle	*(Compare OOL and ULE.)*		

EWER

bluer	booer	brewer	chewer
Clewer	cooer	doer	fewer
hewer	newer	screwer	sewer
skewer	strewer	truer	twoer
viewer	wooer	construer	interviewer
pursuer	renewer	reviewer	

(And compare OOR and URE.)

EWESS

| Jewess | Lewes | Lewis | U.S. |
| St. Louis | | | |

EWISH

| blueish | Jewish | shrewish | twoish |

EWTER, EUTER, UTER, UTOR

| Ceuta | muter | neuter | pewter |
| suitor | tutor | disputer | |

(And further extensions in UTE. Compare OOTER.)

EWY, OUE, UEY

| bluey | coo-ee | Coué | dewy |
| gluey | Jewy | Louie | roué |

EXILE

| exile | flexile |

EXION (see ECTION)

EXOR, EXER

| flexor | *(And extend EX.)* |

EXTANT

| extant | sextant |

EXTILE

| sextile | textile |

EXY

| sexy | apoplexy |

EYANCE, EANCE

seance	abeyance	conveyance	purveyance

IAD

dryad	naiad	hamadryad	jeremiad

IAL, IOL

dial	Dyall	phial	Lyell
trial	vial	viol	decrial
denial	retrial	*(Compare ILE in one-syllable list.)*	

IAN (see EON)

IANCE, IENCE

science	affiance	alliance	appliance
compliance	defiance	reliance	

IANT, IENT

Bryant	client	giant	pliant
compliant	defiant	reliant	self-reliant

IAR

briar	brier	buyer	drier
Dwyer	dyer	friar	fryer
higher	liar	Maria	nigher
plier	prior	pryer	skier
spryer			

*(See under Y in one-syllable rhymes for further extensions
in Y and IGH. Compare IRE.)*

IAS

bias	pious	Ananias	nisi-prius

IAT, IET, IOT

diet	fiat	quiet	riot
ryot	striate	Wyatt	disquiet

IBALD

ribald	*(Extend IBBLE for "quibbled," etc.)*

IBBER

fibber	wine-bibber

(Extend IB for "cribber," etc.)

IBBET, IBIT

gibbet	Tibbett	cohibit	exhibit
inhibit	prohibit		

IBBLE

cribble	dibble	dribble	fribble
nibble	quibble	Ribble	scribble
Sybil			

IBBON

gibbon	ribbon

IBER

fiber	Khyber	Tiber

(And extend IBE for "inscriber," etc.)

IBLE, IBAL

Bible	libel	tribal

IBLET

driblet	giblet	triblet

ICAR   ICKER

bicker	liquor	vicar	*(And extend ICK.)*

ICHEN

lichen	Hitchin	kitchen

ICHES, ITCHES, EECHES

breeches	riches	*(And extend ITCH.)*

ICIAN, ICION, ITION, ISSION

mission	abolition	academician	acquisition
addition	admission	admonition	ambition
ammunition	apparition	apposition	arithmetician
attrition	audition	circuition	circumcision
circumposition	coalition	cognition	coition
commission	competition	composition	condition
contraposition	contrition	decomposition	definition
demolition	dentition	deposition	disparition
disquisition	ebullition	edition	electrician
emission	emolition	erudition	exhibition
expedition	exposition	fruition	geometrician
ignition	imposition	inanition	indisposition
inhibition	inquisition	insition	intermission
interposition	intromission	intuition	juxtaposition
logician	magician	malnutrition	manumission
mathematician	mechanician	metaphysician	monition
munition	musician	nutrition	omission
opposition	optician	partition	parturition
patrician	perdition	permission	petition
physician	politician	position	precognition
predisposition	premonition	preposition	presupposition
preterition	prodition	prohibition	proposition
readmission	recognition	recommission	recomposition
reddition	remission	rendition	repetition
reposition	requisition	rhetorician	sedition
submission	superstition	supposition	suspicion
transition	transmission	transposition	tuition
volition			

ICIOUS, ITIOUS

vicious	adventitious	ambitious	auspicious
avaricious	capricious	cilicious	delicious
factitious	fictitious	flagitious	ignitious
inauspicious	injudicious	judicious	malicious
Mauritius	meretricious	nutritious	officious
pernicious	propitious	seditious	superstitious
supposititious	surreptitious	suspicious	unsuspicious

ICKEN

chicken	quicken	sicken	stricken
thicken	wicken		

123

ICKENING

strychnine   *(And extend words in previous list.)*

ICKER *(see ICAR)*

ICKET

clicket	cricket	picket	piquet
pricket	snicket	spicate	thicket
ticket	wicket	intricate	

(And pluralize some words in this list for "rickets.")

ICKLE, ICKEL

fickle	mickle	nickel	pickle
prickle	sickle	stickle	strickle
tickle	trickle		

ICKLY

quickly	prickly	sickly	slickly
thickly			

ICKSHAW

kickshaw   rickshaw

ICKY

Vicky   *(And extend ICK for "bricky," etc.)*

ICTER, ICTOR

lictor   victor   Victor   boa-constrictor

ICTION, IXION

diction	fiction	friction	addiction
adstriction	affixion	affliction	affriction
astriction	benediction	commixion	constriction
contradiction	conviction	crucifixion	dereliction
eviction	indiction	infliction	interdiction
jurisdiction	malediction	obstriction	prediction
prefixion	restriction	reviction	valediction

ICTURE

picture   stricture   *(And see IXTURE.)*

ICY

icy   spicy

IDAL, IDLE, IDOL

bridal	bridle	idle	idol
idyll	sidle	tidal	fratricidal
homicidal	parricidal	regicidal	suicidal

IDAY *(see IDY)*

IDDEN

bidden	chidden	hidden	midden
ridden	forbidden	unbidden	

IDDISH

kiddish   Yiddish

124

IDDLE

| diddle | fiddle | griddle | middle |
| piddle | riddle | twiddle | tarradiddle |

IDDY

| Biddy | giddy | kiddie | middy |
| skiddy | | | |

IDEN, IDON

| guidon | Sidon | widen | |

IDENT

| guidant | strident | trident | dividant |

IDEOUS

| hideous | fastidious | insidious | invidious |
| lapidious | perfidious | | |

IDER

| cider | Ida | spider | (And extend IDE.) |

IDGET, IGIT

| Bridget | digit | fidget | midget |

IDGY   IDLE (see IDAL)

| midgy | ridgy | | |

IDLY, IDELY

| idly | widely | | |

IDY, IDAY

| Friday | sidy | tidy | bona-fide |

IENCE (see IANCE)   IESTLY (see EASTLY)   IET (see IAT)
IFER, IPHER

| cipher | fifer | lifer | rifer |
| decipher | | | |

IFFER

| biffer | differ | sniffer | |

IFFIN

| Biffen | griffin | tiffin | |

IFFLE

| piffle | whiffle | | |

IFFY

| jiffy | Liffy | niffy | sniffy |
| squiffy | whiffy | | |

IFIC

| beatific | calorific | hieroglyphic | horrific |

pacific	prolific	rubific	scientific
sensific	semnific	soporific	specific
terrific			

IFLE

| eyeful | rifle | stifle | trifle |

IFTER

| drifter | lifter | shifter | sifter |
| snifter | swifter | shop-lifter | |

IFTY

| drifty | fifty | "giftie" | nifty |
| shifty | thrifty | | |

IGATE (see IGOT)

IGEON, IDGEON

| pigeon | Phrygian | Stygian | widgeon |
| religion | irreligion | | |

IGER

| Niger | Riga | tiger | |

IGEST

| digest (*noun*) | obligest | | |

IGGARD, IGGERED, IGURD

| figured | niggard | (*And extend* IGGER.) | |

IGGER, IGOR, IGURE

bigger	digger	figure	jigger
nigger	rigger	rigor	snigger
swigger	trigger	vigor	configure
disfigure	outrigger	transfigure	

IGGIN

| biggin | piggin | | |

IGGISH

| riggish | (*And extend* IG.) | | |

IGGLE

| giggle | higgle | niggle | sniggle |
| squiggle | wriggle | | |

IGGY

| iggy | piggy | twiggy | |

IGHER (see IAR)

IGHLAND

| highland | island | | |

IGHTEN, ITEN

| Brighton | Crichton | triton | |
| (*And extend* ITE *and* IGHT.) | | | |

IGHTER, ITER

miter   niter

(*And extend* ITE, IGHT *and* ITE *for "smiter," "tighter," "triter," etc.*)

IGHTLY

sprightly   (*And extend* ITE *and* IGHT.)

IGHTNING

lightning

(*And extend* IGHTEN *and* ITEN *for "tightening," "whitening," etc.*)

IGHTY

Blighty	Clytie	flighty	mighty
mitey	mightie	whitey	almighty
Aphrodite			

IGIL

sigil   vigil

IGLY, IGGLY

bigly   giggly   sniggly   **wriggly**

IGMA

stigma   enigma

IGMENT

figment   pigment

IGOT, IGATE

bigot   frigate   gigot   **spigot**

IGOUR (*see* IGGER)
IGRESS

digress   tigress

IKEN, ICON

Dicon   icon   liken

IKING

Viking   (*And extend* IKE *for "hiking," etc.*)

IKY

Ikey   crikey   Psyche   **spiky**

ILACS, ILAX

lilacs   smilax

ILBERT

filbert   Gilbert

ILDER

builder	gilder	guilder	Hilda
bewilder	Matilda	St. Kilda	

ILDISH

| childish | mildish | wildish | |

ILFUL

| skilful | wilful | | |

ILIOUS

| bilious | antrabilious | punctilious | supercilious |

ILIGHT

| highlight | skylight | stylite | twilight |

ILKY

| milky | silky | Willkie | |

ILLA

Scylla	villa	chinchilla	gorilla
Manila	sarsaparilla	vanilla	

ILLAGE

| billage | pillage | tillage | village |

ILLAR

| pillar | caterpillar | | |

(And extend ILL for "thriller," etc.)

ILLET

billet	fillet	millet	quillet
rillet	skillet	Willett	

ILLIANT

| brilliant | resilient | | |

ILLIARDS

billiards	chiliads	iliads	milliards
mill-yards			

ILLING

| shilling | *(And extend ILL for "drilling," etc.)* |

ILLION, ILLIAN

billion	Chilean	Gillian	Lillian
million	pillion	trillion	carillon
Castilian	civilian	cotillion	pavilion
postillion	reptilian	vermilion	

ILLOW

billow	kilo	pillow	willow
armadillo	peccadillo		

128

ILLY

billy	Billy	Chile	filly
frilly	gillie	hilly	lily
Lillie	Milly	Scilly	silly
skilly	Willie	Piccadilly	

(And extend ILL for "hilly," etc.)

ILOM

| whilom | asylum | | |

ILTER

filter	gilter	jilter	lilter
milter	philter	quilter	tilter
wilter			

ILY, IGHLY

| Filey | O'Reilly | | |

(And extend Y and IGH for "slily," "highly," etc.)

IMAGE

| image | scrimmage | | |

IMATE

| climate | primate | | |

IMBER

| limber | timber | unlimber | |

IMBLE, YMBAL

cymbal	gimble (*Lewis*	nimble	symbol
thimble	tymbal *Carroll*)	wimble	

IMBO

| limbo | akimbo | | |

IMER

| climber | *(And extend IME for "primer," etc.)* | | |

IMIC

| chymic | mimic | patronymic | |

IMON, YMAN

| flyman | pieman | Simon | Timon |

IMMY

| Jimmy | shimmy | | |

IMPER

| simper | *(And extend IMP for "shrimper," etc.)* | | |

IMPLE

crimple	dimple	pimple	rimple
simple	wimple		

IMSY

| flimsy | "mimsy" (*Lewis Carroll*) | whimsy | |

IMUS

High Mass	primus	thymus	timous

IMY

blimey	grimy	limy	rimy
slimy	thymy	stymie	"gorblimey"

INA

china	Dinah	Carolina	regina

(*Compare* INER).

INAL

final	spinal	trinal

INCERS

mincers	pincers	rinses

INCEST

incest   (*And extend* INCE *for* "wincest," *etc.*)

INCHER

clincher	flincher	pincher

INCTURE

cincture	tincture	vincture

INDER (*short*)

cinder	hinder	tinder

INDER (*long*) (*Extend* IND *for* "blinder," *etc.*)

INDLE

brindle	dwindle	Hindle	kindle
spindle	swindle	windle	rekindle

INDNESS

(*Extend* IND *as in* "kindness.")

INDY

Lindy	shindy	windy

INEAR, INNIER

linear	finnier	skinnier	whinnier

INER, INOR

minor (*And extend* INE *and* IGN *for* "finer," "assigner," *etc.*)
(*Compare* INA.)

INET

ginnet	linnet	minute	spinet

INEW, INUE

sinew	continue	discontinue

130

INFUL

sinful   skinful

INGENT

stringent   astringent   contingent   restringent

INGER

finger   linger *(And extend ING for "singer," etc.)*

INGER *(soft "g")*

ginger   injure *(And extend INGE for "cringer," etc.)*

INGLE

cingle	cringle	dingle	ingle
jingle	mingle	shingle	single
springall	swingle	tingle	surcingle

INGLET

kinglet   ringlet   singlet

INGO

| dingo | gringo | lingo | stingo |
| flamingo | jingo | Domingo | |

INGY

| cringy | dingy. | fringy | mingy |
| stingy | twingy | | |

INIC

actinic   cynic   clinic

INGY *(with hard "g")*

dinghy   springy   stringy

INION, INIAN

| Binyon | minion | Ninian | pinion |
| Carthaginian | dominion | opinion | Virginian |

INIS

finis   Guinness

INISH *(short)*

finish   Finnish   thinnish   diminish

INISH *(long)*

brinish   nineish   swinish

INKLE

| crinkle | sprinkle | tinkle | twinkle |
| winkle | wrinkle | besprinkle | periwinkle |

INKLING and INKY (extend INK)

Helsinki	dinky	slinky

INNER

Pinner (*And extend IN for "dinner," etc.*)

INNOW

minnow	winnow

INNY

finny	guinea	Minnie	ninny
pinny	skinny	spinney	tinny
whinny	Winnie	ignominy	New Guinea

INO

lino	rhino

INSTER

Leinster	minster	Minster	spinster

INSY, INTAGE

linsey	quinsy	mintage	vintage

INTEL

lintel	quintal	pintle

INTER

winter (*And extend INT for "sprinter," etc.*)

INTRY

vintry	wintry

INTY

flinty	minty	squinty	pepperminty

INUS

minus	sinus	spinous	vinous

INY

briny	liny	miny	piney
shiny	spiny	tiny	twiny
winy			

ION

Brian	iron	lion	Lyon
scion	Zion	orion	dandelion

IPED

biped	striped	typed	wiped

IPEND

ripened	stipend

IPER, YPER

viper (*And extend IPE, YPE for "wiper," "typer," etc.*)

IPHON, YPHEN

siphon   hyphen

IPIST, IPEST

typist   (*And extend IPE for "wipest," etc.*)

IPPLE

cripple   nipple   ripple   stipple
tipple   triple

IPLING, IPPLING

Kipling   stripling
  (*And extend IPPLE for "rippling," etc.*)

IPPER, IPPY

kipper   skipper
  (*And extend IP for "clipper," "chippy," etc.*)

IPPET

sippet   snippet   tippet   whippet

IPSTER

tipster   whipster

IPSY

gipsy   "ipse"   tipsy

IPTIC

cryptic   styptic   ecliptic   elliptic

IQUANT

piquant   secant   intersecant

IRANT

tyrant   virant   aspirant   conspirant

IRATE

gyrate   irate   pirate

IRCHEN, URCHIN

birchen   urchin

IRDAR, IRDER, ERDER, URDER

girder   herder   murder   sirdar
absurder

IRDLE, URDLE

curdle   girdle   hurdle

IRDLY

curdly   thirdly   absurdly

IREN

Byron   siren   syren

IRKIN (see ERKIN)

IRLING, ERLING, EARLING, URLING

sterling   Stirling   yearling   whirling
(And extend EARL, IRL, URL.)

IRLISH, URLISH

churlish   girlish

IRLOIN

purloin   sirloin

IRMER, ERMER, URMUR

murmur   (And extend IRM for "firmer," etc.)

IRMISH

firmish   skirmish   squirmish

IRRAH

mirror   sirrah

IRREL

Birrel   Cyril   squirrel   Tyrrell
Tyrol   virile

IRRUP

chirrup   stirrup   syrup

IRTLE, URTLE

hurtle   kirtle   myrtle   Myrtle
spirtle   turtle

IRTY, URTY

Bertie   dirty   flirty   Gertie
shirty   skirty   spurty   squirty
thirty

IRUS

virus   desirous

IRY, IARY, IERY

briery   diary   fiery   miry
priory   spiry   wiry   enquiry

ISCARD

discard   Liscard

ISCOUNT
discount   miscount

ISCUIT (see ISKET)

ISCUS
discus   viscous

ISECT
bisect   trisect

ISER, ISOR
Kaiser   miser   sizar   visor
incisor   *(And extend* ISE *for "advisor," etc.)*

ISHER, ISSURE
disher   fisher   fissure   wisher

ISHOP
bishop   fish-shop

ISIC
Chiswick   phthisic   physic   metaphysic

ISION, ISSION
scission	vision	abscission	allision
circumcision	collision	decision	derision
division	ellision	Elysian	excision
incision	misprision	precision	prevision
provision	recision	rescission	revision
subdivision	television		

(For rhymes to "mission" see ICIAN.)

ISIS
crisis   Isis   phthisis
(And compare plurals of ICE.)

ISIT
visit   exquisite

ISKER
brisker   frisker   risker   whisker

ISKET
biscuit   brisket   wisket

ISKY
frisky   risky   whisky

ISLY, IZZLY

Bisley	drizzly	frizzly	grisly
grizzly			

ISMAL

dismal	abysmal	baptismal

ISON (*see* IZZEN)

ISPER

crisper	lisper	whisper

ISSAL (*see* ISTLE)   **ISSION** (*see* ICIAN)

ISSUE

issue	fichu	tissue	atishoo

ISSURE (*see* ISHER)
ISTANCE

distance	assistance	co-existence	consistence
equidistance	existence	inconsistence	insistence
non-existence	non-resistance	resistance	subsistence

ISTANT (*adapt previous list for* "distant," *etc.*)

ISTEN

christen	glisten	listen

ISTER

bister	blister	glister	mister
sister	twister		

ISTHMUS (*see* ISTMAS)

ISTIC

cystic	fistic	mystic	anarchistic
atheistic	bolshevistic	cabalistic	characteristic
communistic	deistic	fascistic	pantheistic
polytheistic	socialistic	syllogistic	theistic
tritheistic			

ISTINE

Christine	pristine	amethystine

ISTLE, ISSAL

bristle	gristle	missal	missel
missile	thistle	whistle	dismissal
epistle			

ISTMAS

Christmas	isthmus

ISTOL

Bristol	crystal	pistol

ITAL

title	vital	entitle	marital
recital	requital	subtitle	

ITER

miter   niter
(And extend ITE *and* IGHT *for "biter," "lighter," etc.)*

ITHER *(short)*

blither	dither	hither	slither
thither	whither	wither	zither

ITHER *(long) (see* EITHER *with "i" sounded)*

ITIAN

titian   *(And see rhymes in* ICIAN. *Compare* ISION.)

ITIC

critic	hypercritic	hypocritic	mephitic
politic	syphilitic		

ITISH, ITTISH

British	fittish	kittish	skittish

ITNESS

fitness   witness

ITTANCE

pittance   *(And extend* IT *for "quittance," "admittance," etc.)*

ITTED, ITIED
(Extend IT *und* ITTY *for "pitted," "pitied," etc.)*

ITTEN

bitten	Briton	kitten	mitten
smitten	Witan	written	Thames Ditton

ITTER

bitter	"crittur"	fitter	flitter
fritter	glitter	hitter	knitter
litter	pitter	quitter	sitter
slitter	spitter	splitter	titter
twitter	*(And extend* IT *for "transmitter," etc.)*		

ITTLE, ITTAL, ICTUAL

brittle	knittle	little	quittal
skittle	spittle	tittle	victual

| whittle | wittol | acquittal | belittle |
| committal | transmittal | | |

ITTY

chitty	city	ditty	gritty
Kitty	nitty	pity	pretty
witty	banditti	committee	

ITUAL

| ritual | habitual | | |

IVAL

| rival | (And extend IVE for "arrival," etc.) | | |

IVEL, IVIL

| civil | drivel | rivel | shrivel |
| snivel | swivel | uncivil | |

IVEN

| driven | given | riven | shriven |
| striven | wivern | | |

IVER (short)

"flivver"	giver	liver	quiver
river	shiver	sliver	deliver
Guadalquivir			

IVER (long)

fiver	Ivor	stiver	saliva
Lady Godiva			
(And extend IVE for "diver," etc.)			

IVET, IVIT

| civet | privet | rivet | trivet |
| Glenlivet | (Compare IVOT.) | | |

IVID

| chivvied | livid | vivid | |

IVOT

| divot | pivot | (Compare IVET.) | |

IVY (short)

| civvy | chivy | Livy | privy |
| skivvy | tantivy | (No rhyme for "ivy.") | |

IXIE

| dixie | Dixie | pixy | tricksy |
| Trixie | | | |

IXER, IXIR

| elixir | (And extend IX for "fixer," etc.) | | |

IXTURE

| fixture | mixture | admixture | commixture |

IZARD, IZZARD, ISSORED

bizard	blizzard	gizzard	Izzard
lizard	scissored	vizard	wizard

IZZEN, IZEN, ISON

mizzen	prison	wizen	bedizen
imprison	(*Compare* ISTEN.)		

IZON and ISON (*long*)

bison	horizon

IZZIER

busier	dizzier	fizzier	frizzier
vizier			

IZZLE

chisel	drizzle	fizzle	frizzle
grizzle	mizzle	sizzle	

IZZLING

quisling	(*And extend above as in "drizzling."*)

IZZY, USY

busy	dizzy	fizzy	frizzy
Lizzie	mizzy	tizzy	

OA

boa	Goa	moa	Noah
poa	proa	Genoa	Iowa
jerboa	Samoa		

OADER, ODOR

odor
(*And extend OAD, ODE for "loader," "exploder," etc.*)
(*Compare* ODA.)

OAFY

feoffee	loafy	oafy	Sophie
strophe	trophy		

OAKER, OKER, OCHRE

ochre   Roker
(*And extend OAK and OKE for "soaker," "joker," etc.*)

OAKUM, OCUM

hokum	locum	oakum	Slocum

OALY, OLY, OLEY, OLLY (*long*), OWLY

coaly	Crowley	drolly	goalie
holey	holy	lowly	moly
Rowley	shoaly	slowly	wholly
roly-poly			

OAMER

comber	Cromer	foamer	Homer

O

omer   roamer   misnomer
   (*Compare* OMA.)

OANER, ONER, ONOR, OWNER

donor	loaner	loner	moaner
Mona	owner	postponer	stoner
atoner	Corona	deponer	intoner
telephoner	Arizona	deponer	

   (*Compare* ONA.)

OAPY

mopy   soapy   topee

OARISH

boarish   whorish   (*Compare* OORISH.)

OARSER

| coarser | courser | forcer | hawser |
| hoarser | | | |

   (*Compare* AUCER.)

OARY, ORY

dory	glory	gory	hoary
lory	more (*Latin*)	storey	story
Tory	furore		

OASTAL, OSTAL

coastal   postal

OASTER, OSTER (*Extend* OAST *and* OST *for* "coaster," "poster," *etc.*)

OATBRIDGE

boat-bridge   Coatbridge   moat-bridge

OATER, OTER, OTOR

bloater   motor   (*And extend* OAT *and* OTE.)
   (*Compare* OTA.)

OBBER

clobber   slobber   swabber   (*And extend* OB.)

OBBIN

bobbin   Dobbin   robin   Robin

OBBLE

| cobble | gobble | hobble | nobble |
| squabble | wobble | (*Add* "r" *for* "cobbler," *etc.*) | |

OBBY

| bobby | Bobby | hobby | knobby |
| lobby | mobby | nobby | Robbie |

OBELESS, OBLESSE

noblesse   robeless

OBER

prober	rober	sober	**October**

OBOE

hobo	oboe	Launcelot Gobbo (*"Merchant of Venice"*)

OCAL

focal	local	phocal	**vocal**

OCEAN (*see* OTION)

OCER, OSER, OSSER

closer	grocer	engrosser	(*Extend* OSE.)

OCHRE (*see* OAKER)

OCKADE

blockade	brocade	cockade	**dock-aid**
okayed	stockade		

OCKER

cocker   soccer   knickerbocker
(*And extend* OCK *for "shocker," etc.*)

OCKET

brocket	docket	locket	**pocket**
rocket	socket	sprocket	**pickpocket**

OCKNEY

cockney	knock-knee

OCKY

cocky	crocky	hockey	**jockey**
rocky	stocky		

OCOA, OCO, OKO

boko	cocoa	toko	**Orinoco**
rococo			

OCTION (*see* AUCTION)

OCTOR

doctor	proctor	concocter	**decocter**

OCUM (*see* OAKUM)

OCUS

crocus	**focus**	hocus	**locus**
trochus	hocus-pocus		

141

OCUST

focused   hocused   locust

ODA

| coda | Rhoda | soda | Baroda |
| pagoda | Fashoda | (*Compare* OADER.) | |

ODDEN

Flodden   sodden   trodden   untrodden

ODDER

| codder | dodder | fodder | nodder |
| odder | plodder | prodder | |

ODDESS, ODICE

bodice   goddess

ODDEST, ODEST

bodiced   modest (*And extend* ODD *for* "oddest," *etc.*)

ODDLE, ODEL

| coddle | model | noddle | swaddle |
| toddle | waddle | yodel | |

ODDY, ODY

body	cloddy	noddy	shoddy
toddy	busybody	embody	Irrawaddy
Tom Noddy			

ODGER

dodger   codger   lodger   stodger

ODGY

podgy   splodgy   stodgy

ODIC

| odic | episodic | periodic | spasmodic |
| synodic | | | |

ODIUM

odium   podium   sodium   allodium

ODOR (*see* OADER)

ODUS

modus   nodus

OEM, OET

poem   proem   poet   inchoate

OEY

| blowy | Bowie | Chloe | doughy |
| goey | Joey | snowy | showy |

OFA

| chauffeur | gopher | loafer | sofa |

OFFEE

| coffee | toffee |

OFFER

| coffer | cougher | doffer | golfer |
| offer | proffer | scoffer | |

OFTEN, OFTENER

| often | soften | oftener | softener |

OFTY

| lofty | softy |

OGEY

| bogey | fogey | Yogi |

OGGISH

| doggish | froggish | hoggish |

OGGLE

| boggle | coggle | goggle | joggle |
| toggle | | | |

OGGY

boggy	cloggy	doggy	foggy
froggie	groggy	joggy	moggie
soggy			

OGLE

| bogle | ogle |

OGRESS

| ogress | progress |

OIC

| stoic | heroic | azoic | diapnoic |

0

OIDER

| moider | avoider | embroider |

OILY

| coyly | doily | oily |
(*Compare* "loyally" *and* "royally.")

OINER

| coiner | joiner | purloiner | Moyna |

OINTMENT

| ointment | (*And extend* OINT.) |

OISTER, OYSTER

| cloister | foister | hoister | moister |
| oyster | roister | | |

OITER

| goiter | loiter | Ruyter | adroiter |

exploiter

OKAY

| bouquet | okay | Tokay | Touquet |

OKEN, OAKEN

| token | betoken | (And extend OAK and OKE.) |

OKEY

| chokey | croquet | joky | oaky |
| poky | smoky | trochee | |

OLAR, OLLER, OWLER

bowler	droller	molar	polar
roller	solar	stroller	toller
comptroller	condoler	consoler	controller
enroller			

OLDEN

| ~olden | olden | beholden | embolden |

OLDER, OULDER

| boulder | molder | shoulder | smolder |
| (And extend OLD for "folder," etc.) | | | |

OLEFUL

| ɔwlful | doleful | soulful |

OLEMN, OLUMN

| column | solemn |

OLEN, OLON

| colon | Nolan | solen | solon |
| stolen | swollen | semi-colon | |

OLIC, OLLICK

colic	frolic	rollick	alcoholic
apostolic	bucolic	carbolic	diabolic
hyperbolic	melancholic	parabolic	vitriolic
(Compare AULIC.)			

OLID

| dollied | jollied | solid | squalid |
| stolid | volleyed | | |

OLISH, OLLISH

| dollish | polish | abolish | demolish |

OLIUM

| scholium | linoleum | petroleum |

OLLAR, OLAR, OLER

| choler | collar | dollar | dolor |
| scholar | squalor | Waller | |

OLLARD, OLLARED

| bollard | collared | dollared | Lollard |
| pollard | "scholard" | | |

144

OLLEGE, OWLEDGE

college	knowledge	acknowledge

OLLET

collet	wallet

OLLIER

collier	jollier

OLLOP

collop	dollop	gollop	lollop
scollop	trollop	wallop	

OLLOW

follow	hollow	Rollo	swallow
wallow	Apollo		

OLLY, OLLEY

brolly	collie	dolly	Dolly
folly	golly	holly	jolly
Molly	Polly	Solly	trolley
volley	melancholy		

OLO

bolo	polo	solo

OLSTER

bolster	holster	oldster	upholster

OLORED

colored	dullard

OLTER, OULTER

bolter	colter	jolter	molter
poulter	revolter		

OLTEST, OULTICED

poulticed (*And extend OLT for "joltest," etc.*)

OLTISH

coltish	doltish

OLUMN (*see* OLEMN) OLY (*see* OALY)

OMA

coma	soma	Roma	aboma
aroma	diploma	Tacoma	

(*Compare* OAMER.)

OMACH, UMMOCK

hummock stomach (*Add "s" to rhyme with "flummox."*)

OMAIN

domain	ptomaine

OMAN, OWMAN

| bowman | foeman | gnomon | Roman |
| showman | snow-man | yeoman | |

OMBAT

| combat | wombat | | |

OMBER

| bomber | omber | somber | |

OMEN

omen (*And pluralise words under* OMAN; *thus* "bowmen."*)

OMENT

| foment (*noun*) | loment | moment | |

OMET, OMIT

| comet | vomit | Mahomet | |

OMIC

| comic | atomic | astronomic | economic |
| gnomic | | | |

OMING, UMBING, UMMING

| coming | plumbing | | |

(*And extend* UM *for* "humming," *etc.*)

OMMY

| Tommy | bonhomie | consommé | Dahomey |

OMPASS

| compass | rumpus | encompass | |

OMPTER

| compter | prompter | accompter | |

ONA

donar	Jonah	Mona	Arizona
Catriona	corona		Iona
Verona	(*Compare* OANER.)		

ONAGE

| nonage | Swanage | | |

ONDANT, ONDENT

| fondant | despondent | correspondent | respondent |

ONDEL, ONDLE

| Blondel | fondle | rondle | Wandle |

ONDER

| blonder | bonder | condor | fonder |
| ponder | squander | wander | yonder |

(*Extend* OND *for* "absconder," *etc.*)

ONELY

lonely	only

ONEST

connest	donnest	honest	wannest
non est			

ONGER

conger	longer	stronger	Tonga
wronger			

ONGO

Congo	pongo

ONIC

chronic	conic	tonic	adonic
alcyonic	Byronic	carbonic	diatonic
embryonic	euphonic	gramophonic	harmonic
histrionic	ionic	ironic	laconic
macaronic	microphonic	mnemonic	platonic
Slavonic	symphonic	telephonic	Teutonic

ONION (see UNION)

ONISH, ONNISH

donnish	admonish	astonish	premonish

ONKY, ONKEY

conky	donkey	wonky

ONKEY (as in "monkey," see UNKY)

ONNAGE, UNNAGE

dunnage	Dunwich	tonnage

ONNET

bonnet	sonnet

ONNY

bonny	Johnny	Connie	nonny
Ronnie			

ONOR, ONER

goner	honor	wanner	dishonor

ONSIL, ONSUL

consul	sponsal	tonsil	proconsul
responsal			

ONTEST, ONTRACT

contest	wantest	contract	entr'acte

ONY, ONEY

bony	cony	coney	crony

O

drony	phoney	pony	stony
tony	Tony	boloney	macaroni
Marconi	polony		

ONYX

onyx   phonics

OOBY

booby   looby   ruby   Ruby

OODLE

boodle	feudal	noodle	poodle
doodle	caboodle	canoodle	flapdoodle
Yankee-Doodle			

OODY (*short*)

goodie   roody   woody

OODY (*long*)

broody   Judy   moody

OOKISH

bookish   flukish   rookish   spookish

OOKY (*short*)

bookie   cookie   hookey   rookie

OOKY (*long*)

fluky   spooky   Sukie

OOLISH, ULISH, OOMY, UMY (*extend* OOL, ULE, OOM *and* UME)

OONER (*see* UNAR)   OONFUL (*see* UNEFUL)

OONY, UNY

pruny   puisne   puny   tuny
(*And extend* OON *for "loony," etc.*)

OOPER, UPER, UPOR

Cupar   super   stupor
(*And extend* OOP *for "cooper," etc.*)

OOPY, OUPY

| croupy | droopy | loopy | rupee |
| soupy | whoopee | whoopy | |

OORISH

boorish	Moorish	poorish

OOSER, USER
(Extend OOSE and USE, etc., for "chooser," "bruiser," "loser," "user," etc.)

OOTER

freebooter
(And extend OOT for "hooter," etc. Compare EWTER.)

OOTLE

Bootle	brutal	footle	tootle
refutal			

OOTY

beauty	booty	cutie	dhooti
duty	fluty	fruity	rooty
sooty			

OOVER

groover	prover	maneuver	Vancouver

(And extend OOVE and OVE for "hoover," "remover," etc.)

OOZLE, OUSEL, USIL

foozle	fusil	ousel	bamboozle
perusal	refusal		

OOZY

boozy	newsy	oozy

OPAL

Bhopal	copal	opal	Adrianople
Constantinople			

OPER (short), OPPER

Dopper	Joppa	proper	improper
toper			

(And extend OP for "shopper," "topper," etc.)

OPER (long), OAPER

sloper	Soper	toper

(And extend OAP and OPE for "soaper," "moper," etc.)

OPHET

profit	prophet	Tophet

OPHIST

officed	sophist

(And extend OFF for "doffest," etc.)

149

OPIC

topic tropic

(*And extend* OPE *for "microscopic," etc.*)

OPISH

mopish Popish

OPLAR, OPLING

poplar toppler fopling toppling

OPPY (*short*)

copy Poppy (*And extend* OP *for "floppy," etc.*)

OPSY

dropsy topsy Topsy autopsy

OPTIC

Coptic optic synoptic

OPTION

option adoption

OPY (*long*), OAPY

soapy topee (*And extend* OPE *for "mopy," etc.*)

ORA

aura Cora Dora flora
Flora Laura Norah Kiora
Andorra Aurora

(*And compare extensions of* OAR *and* ORE *as in "roarer" and "snorer."*)

ORAGE

borage forage porridge

ORAL (*short*)

coral laurel moral quarrel
sorrel Balmoral immoral unmoral

ORAL (*long*)

aural choral floral horal
oral thoral binaural femoral

ORAN

Koran moron

ORAX

borax storax thorax

ORBEL

bauble corbel warble

ORCHARD, ORCHER

orchard tortured lorcha scorcher
torture

ORDER, OARDER

Cawdor Lauder order warder

(And extend words under OARD Thus "hoarder," "re-corder," etc.)

ORDIAL, ORDEAL

cordial ordeal primordial

ORDLING

dawdling lordling maudlin

ORDON

Bordon cordon Gordon Jordan
warden

ORDSHIP

lordship wardship

OREAL, ORIAL

boreal oriel ambassadorial armorial
conspiratorial dictatotial equatorial immemorial
inquisitorial memorial pictorial senatorial

OREIGN, ORIN

foreign florin sporran warren

ORELOCK

forelock Porlock warlock

ORENCE

Florence Lawrence torrents abhorrence

OREST, ORIST

forest florist

ORGAN

gorgon Morgan organ Glamorgan

ORGER

Borgia forger gorger disgorger

ORGI, ORGY

Corgi Georgie orgy

ORIC

choric chloric doric Warwick
Yorrick allegoric categoric historic
metaphoric paregoric

151

ORID, ORRID

forehead	florid	horrid	quarried
torrid			

ORIS

Boris	Doris	Horace	loris
morris	Norris	deoch-an-doras	(often misspelled as "dock and doris")

ORKY

corky	door-key	porky

(Compare AWKY.)

ORMAL

formal	normal	abnormal

ORMAN

doorman	foreman	Mormon	Norman
storeman	longshoreman		

ORMANT

dormant	torment	informant

ORMER

dormer	Walmer	warmer

(And extend ORM for "former," etc.)

ORNER

corner	Lorna	pawner	scorner
warner	yawner	suborner	

(Compare OURNER.) (Extend AWN for "spawner," etc.)

ORNET

cornet	hornet

ORNING, AWNING

awning	mourning

(And extend AWN and ORN for "dawning," "morning," etc.)

ORNY

corny	horny	Pawnee	thorny

(Compare AWNY.)

OROUGH

borough	thorough	(Compare URROW)

ORPOR, AUPER

pauper	torpor	warper

ORPUS

corpus	porpoise	habeas corpus

ORRAL, ORREL (see ORAL, short)

ORRENT

torrent warrant abhorrent

ORRID (*see* ORID)

ORROR

horror abhorrer

ORROW

borrow morrow Morro sorrow

ORRY

Florrie Laurie lorry quarry
soirée sorry (For rhymes to *"worry,"* see URRY.)

ORSAL, ORSEL

dorsal foresail morsel torsal

ORSET

corset Dorset

ORSTED, IRSTED

thirsted worsted

ORTAGE

cortege portage

ORTAL, ORTLE

chortle mortal portal tortile
aortal immortal

ORTAR, ORTER

mortar quarter

(*Extend* ORT *for "porter," etc., and compare* AUGHTER.)

ORTEN

quarten Morton Norton shorten
Wharton

ORTION

portion torsion abortion apportion
(*Extend* ORT *for "contortion," etc., and compare*
AUTION.)

ORTLY, OURTLY

courtly (*And extend* ORT *for "portly," etc.*)

153

ORTIVE

sportive   tortive   abortive

ORTRESS

court-dress   fortress   portress

ORTUNE

fortune   importune   misfortune

ORTURE (see ORCHER)

ORTY

forte	forty	porty	rorty
snorty	sortie	sporty	warty

(*Compare* AUGHTY.)

ORUM

forum	jorum	quorum	Shoreham
ad valorem	cockalorem	decorum	indecorum
pons asinorum			

ORUS, AURUS

aurous	chorus	chlorous	porous
taurus	canorous	decorous	imporous
sonorous			

ORWAY   OSEN (see OZEN, *long*)

doorway   Norway

OSET, OSIT

closet   posit   posset   deposit

OSHER

cosher	Kosher	posher	swasher
washer			

OSIER, OSURE

cosier	crozier	dozier	hosier
osier	nosier	rosier	

(*And extend* OSE *for "closure," etc.*)

OSKY

bosky   drosky

OSMIC

cosmic   osmic

OSSACKS

Cossacks   Trossachs

OSSAGE
Osage   bossage   sausage

OSSER
bosser   dosser   josser   prosser
tosser   embosser

OSSUM
blossom   oppossum

OSSY
Flossie   (*And extend OSS for "bossy," etc.*)

OSTAL (*short*), OSTEL
costal   hostel   postil   pentecostal

OSTAL (*long*) (*see* OASTAL)

OSTER (*long*) (*see* OASTER)

OSTER (*short*)
coster   foster   Gloucester   accoster
paternoster

OSTESS
ghostess   hostess

OSTIC
caustic   gnostic   joss-stick   accostic
agnostic   diagnostic   prognostic

OSTLE, OSSIL
dossil   fossil   jostle   throstle
wassail   apostle

OSTLER
hostler   jostler   ostler   wassailer

OSTLY, OSTREL
ghostly   mostly   costrel   nostril

OSTRUM   OSURE (*see* OZIER)
nostrum   rostrum

OSY, OZY
cosy   dozy   nosy   posy
prosy   rosy   Rosie

OTA
quota   rota   Bogota   Dakota
iota   Minnesota   (*Compare* OATER.)

OTAL

dotal	total	anecdotal	antidotal
sacerdotal	teetotal		

OTARD

dotard	motored

OTCHER

botcher	notcher	watcher	top-notcher

OTER, OTOR (*see* OATER)

OTHER

bother	pother

OTHER (*as in "mother"*)

brother	mother	smother	other
another	Anstruther		

OTIC

azotic	chaotic	despotic	erotic
exotic	hypnotic	idiotic	nepotic
patriotic	quixotic		

OTION, OCEAN

lotion	motion	notion	ocean
potion	commotion	devotion	emotion
locomotion	promotion		

OTIVE

motive	votive	locomotive

OTLY

hotly	motley	Otley	squatly

OTNESS

hotness	Totness

OTTAGE

cottage	pottage	wattage

OTTEN, OTTON

cotton	"hot 'un" (*And extend* OT *for "rotten," etc.*)

OTTER, OTA

ottar	otter	cottar	squatter
swatter	(*And extend* OT *for "hotter," etc.*)		

OTTISH

Scottish	schottische	sottish

OTTLE, OTTEL

bottle	dottel	mottle	pottle
throttle	wattle		

OTTO

blotto	grotto	motto	Otto
ridotto	Watteau	what ho!	

OTTY

Lottie	Totty	(*And extend* OT *for "dotty," etc.*)

OTUM, OTEM

pro tem	quotum	totem

OUBLE, UBBLE

bubble	double	rubble	stubble
trouble			

OUBLET

doublet	sub-let

OUCHER

coucher	poucher	voucher

OUDER (*see* OWDER)

OUGHTY (*see* AUGHTY *and* OUTY)

OUGHBOY   OUGHBOY (*with "o" sounded*)

cowboy	ploughboy	doughboy	hautboy

OULDER (*see* OLDER)   OUNDER (*extend* OUND)

OUNSEL

council	counsel	groundsel

OUNTAIN

fountain	mountain

OUNTY

bounty	county	"mounty" (*Canadian*)

OUNTER

encounter	rencounter

(And extend OUNT *for "mounter," "discounter," etc.)*

OURAGE

borage	courage	demurrage	discourage
encourage			

OURISH

| currish | flourish | nourish | |

OURNEY, ERNY

| Burney | Czerny | Ernie | ferny |
| journey | tourney | attorney | |

OUSAL

| housel | tousle | carousal | espousal |

OUSER (*see* OWSER)   OUSIN (*see* OZEN)

OUSY, OWZY

| blowzy | drowsy | frowsy | lousy |
| mousy | | | |

OUTY, OUGHTY

| doughty | droughty | flouty | gouty |
| pouty | snouty | sprouty | |

OVEL

| grovel | hovel | novel | |

OVEL (*as in "shovel"*)

| Lovel | shovel | | |

OVEN (*short*)

| covin | oven | sloven | |

OVEN (*long*)

| cloven | proven | woven | interwoven |

OVER (*short*)

| cover | glover | lover | plover |
| shover | discover | recover | |

OVER (*long*)

clover	Dover	drover	over
rover	stover	trover	moreover
half-seas-over			

OVETAIL

| dovetail | love-tale | | |

158

OWAGE

stowage   towage

OWARD, OWERED

coward   Howard *(And extend OWER for "flowered," etc.)*

OWDER, OUDER

chowder	crowder	louder	powder
prouder			

OWDY

cloudy   dowdy   rowdy

OWEL

bowel	Powell	rowel	towel
trowel	vowel	disembowel	*(Compare OWL.)*

OWER (as in "mower")
(Extend OW and OWE for "crower," "ower," etc.) (Compare OUR.)

OWER (as in "bower")

bower	cower	dower	flower
Giaour	lower	power	shower
tower	endower	overpower	

OWLEDGE (see OLLEGE)

OWLER (as in "bowler," see OLAR)

OWLER, OULER

fouler   **(And extend OWL for "fowler," etc.)**

OWMAN (see OMAN)
OWNSMAN

gownsman   roundsman   townsman

OWNY, OWNIE

brownie	browny	downy	Rowney
towny			

OWRY, OWERY, OURI

bowery	Bowery	cowry	dowry
floury	houri	*(And extend OWER for "flowery," etc.)*	

OWSER

Bowser	browser	dowser	grouser
Mauser	mouser	rouser	towser
trouser	carouser	espouser	

159

OWY

blowy	Chloe	doughy	goey
Joey	showy	snowy	

OXEN

cockswain	oxen	Oxon

OXY

doxy	foxy	poxy	proxy
heterodoxy	orthodoxy		

OYAL

loyal	royal	disloyal	(Compare OIL.)

OYANT

buoyant	clairvoyant

OYLY (see OILY)

OZEN (short), OUSIN

cousin	cozen	dozen

OZEN (long), OSEN

boatswain	chosen	frozen	squozen

OZZLE, OSEL

losel	nozzle	sozzle	schemozzle
schnozzle			

UAL (see UEL)

UANT

fluent	truant	diluent	pursuant

UAVE

suave	Zouave

UBA

Cuba	tuba

UBBER

slubber	indiarubber	landlubber

(And extend UB for "rubber," etc.)

UBBERED

blubbered   cupboard   Hubbard   rubbered

UBBISH

cubbish   clubbish   grubbish   rubbish
tubbish

UBBLE (see OUBLE)

UBBLY

bubbly   doubly   knubbly   rubbly
stubbly

UBBY

cubby   chubby   grubby   hubby
scrubby   shrubby   stubby   tubby

UBIC

cubic   cherubic

UBLISH

bubblish   publish

UBY (see OOBY)   UCCOUR (see UCKER)

UCENT

lucent   recusant   reducent   translucent

UCID

deuced   loosed   lucid   mucid
pellucid

UCKER

succor   (*And extend UCK for "mucker," etc.*)

UCKET

bucket   tucket   Nantucket

UCKLE

buckle   chuckle   huckle   knuckle
muckle   stuckle   suckle   truckle
honeysuckle   unbuckle

UCKLER

swashbuckler   (*And extend UCKLE.*)

UCKLING

duckling   (*And extend UCKLE for "buckling," etc.*)

161

U

UCKLED

cuckold   (And extend UCKLE for "buckled," etc.)

UCKY

ducky   Kentucky (And extend UCK for "mucky," etc.)

UCRE

eucher   fluker   lucre   snooker
rebuker

UCTION, UXION

fluxion	ruction	suction	abduction
affluxion	construction	deduction	defluxion
destruction	effluxion	induction	instruction
introduction	misconstruction	obstruction	production
reduction	reproduction	seduction	superstruction
superinduction			

UDDER

"brudder"   dudder   flooder   rudder
scudder   shudder   udder

UDDING

hooding   pudding   wooding

UDDLE

cuddle   fuddle   huddle   muddle
puddle   ruddle

UDDY

bloody   buddy   cuddy   muddy
ruddy   studdy   study

UDENT

prudent   student   concludent   imprudent

UDER, UDOR

Tudor   (And extend UDE for "rude" etc.)

UDGEON

bludgeon   dudgeon   gudgeon   trudgeon
curmudgeon

UDISH

blue-dish   crudish   dudish   lewdish
new dish   nudish   prudish   rudish
stew-dish

162

UDIST

crudest	feudist	lewdest	nudest
nudist			

UEL

crewel	cruel	dual	duel
Ewell	fuel	gruel	jewel
renewal	ruelle	(*Compare* OOL *and* ULE.)	

UENT (*see* UANT)   UEY (*see* EWY)

UET

chuet	cruet	Hewett	suet

UFFER

buffer	duffer	suffer
(*And extend* UFF *and* OUGH.)		

UFFIN

muffin	puffin	ragamuffin

UFFLE

buffel	duffel	muffle	ruffle
scuffle	shuffle	snuffle	truffle

UFFLY and UFFY (*extend* UFF *and* OUGH)

mufti	tufty

UFTY, UFTI

UGAL, UGLE

bugle	frugal	centrifugal	McDougall

UGGER

rugger	(*And extend* UG *for* "lugger," *etc.*)

UGGLE

guggle	juggle	smuggle	snuggle
struggle	(*Add* "r" *for* "juggler," *etc.*)		

UGGY

buggy	muggy	puggy	sluggy

UGLY

smugly	snugly	ugly

UICY

goosey	juicy	Lucy	saucy
Debussy	retroussé		

UID

druid	fluid

163

U

UIN
bruin ruin Trewin

UISANCE
nuisance usance

ULCER
ulcer repulser

ULGAR
Bulgar fulgor vulgar

ULGENT
fulgent effulgent emulgent indulgent

ULKY
bulky hulky sulky

ULLAH
mullah nullah Abdulla (*Compare* ULLER.)

ULLARD
dullard colored

ULLER, OLOR
color culler duller sculler
discolor medulla (*Compare* ULLAH.)

ULLET (*as in "bullet"*) ULLET (*as in "gullet"*)
bullet pullet gullet mullet

ULLION
mullion scullion rapscallion

ULLY (*as in "fully"*)
bully fully pulley woolly
(*And many false rhymes in adverbs ending in ULLY, thus "beautifully."*)

ULLY (*as in "gully"*)
cully dully gully hully
sully Tully

ULPIT
bull-pit pulpit

ULSION

compulsion	convulsion	emulsion	expulsion
impulsion	propulsion	repulsion	revulsion

ULSIVE (*adapt words in previous list for "impulsive," etc.*)

ULTRY

sultry   adult'ry

ULTURE

culture	multure	sculpture	vulture
agriculture	horticulture	sepulture	

ULU

Lulu   pulu   Zulu

ULY, UELY, EWLY, OOLIE, OOLY

bluely	coolie	coolly	duly
Julie	newly	ruly	truly
viewly	unduly	unruly	untruly

UMA

Duma   puma   Montezuma
   (*Compare UMOR.*)

UMAGE

fumage   plumage   roomage

UMAN

cueman	Crewe-man	crewman	human
Kew-man	Krooman	Newman	pew-man
woman	ichneumon	inhuman	

UMBAR, UMBER

cumber	Humber	lumbar	lumber
number	Rumba	slumber	umber
cucumber	encumber	outnumber	

UMBER (*soft "b"*), UMMER

comer   dumber   summer
   (*And extend UM for "drummer," etc.*)

UMBLE

bumble	crumble	dumb-bell	fumble
grumble	humble	jumble	mumble
rumble	scumble	stumble	tumble

UMBLY, OMELY

comely	crumbly	dumbly	grumly
humbly	numbly		

(*Also Cholmondeley, pronounced "chumley."*)

U

UMBRIL

tumbril   umbril

UMID

fumid   humid   plum*ed*   tumid
exhum*ed* perfum*ed*

UMMIT

plummet   summit

UMMY

chummy   crummy   dummy   gummy
lummy   mummy   rummy   slummy
tummy

UMOR, UMER, OOMER

bloomer   humor   rumor   stumer
tumor   (*And extend* OOM *and* UME.)

UMOUS

fumous   glumous   grumous   humus
plumous   spumous   strumous

UMPET

crumpet   strumpet   trumpet

UMPISH *and* UMPY (*extend* UMP)

UMPKIN

bumpkin   lumpkin   pumpkin

UMPLE

crumple   rumple

UMPTION

gumption   sumption   assumption   consumption
presumption resumption

UMPTIOUS

bumptious   gumptious   scrumptious   assumptious

UMPUS, OMPASS

compass   rumpus   encompass

UNAR, UNER, OONER

lunar   Poonah   schooner   Una
icjuner
    (*And extend* OON, UNE, *for* "crooner," "tuner," *etc.*)

UNBURNT

sunburnt   unburnt

UNCHEON

luncheon   nuncheon   puncheon   truncheon
Asuncion

UNKLE

Funchal   truncal   uncle   carbuncle
siphuncle

UNCTION

function   junction   unction   compunction
conjunction   defunction   disjunction   expunction
injunction   subjunction

UNCTURE

juncture   puncture   conjuncture   compuncture

UNDAY, UNDY

Monday   Grundy (*Mrs.*)   Lundy   Sunday

UNDER

blunder   dunder   plunder   sunder
thunder   wonder   asunder   fecunder
jocunder   refunder   rotunder   thereinunder

UNDLE

bundle   Blundell   rundle   trundle

UNEFUL

spoonful   tuneful

UNGER (*soft* "g")

lunger   plunger   sponger   spunger

UNGER (*hard* "g")

hunger   monger   younger   costermonger
fishmonger   ironmonger

UNGLE

bungle   jungle

UNIC

| punic | Munich | runic | tunic |

UNION (*as in "bunion"*)

| bunion | Bunyan | onion | ronion |
| trunnion | | | |

UNION (*as in "union"*)

| union | communion | disunion | reunion |

UNIOR

| junior | punier | spoonier | tunier |

UNISH, UNNISH (*Extend UN for "punish," "Hunnish," etc.*)
UNKARD, UNKERED

| bunkered | drunkard |

UNKEN

| drunken | Duncan | shrunken | sunken |

UNKER

| Junker | punkah | (*Extend UNK for "bunker," etc.*) |

UNKET

| junket | plunket |

UNKY

| flunkey | funky | hunky | monkey |
| nunky | spunky | trunky | |

UNLIT

| sunlit | unlit |

UNNAGE

| dunnage | Dunwich | Hun-age | nonage |
| tonnage | | | |

UNNEL

| funnel | gunwale | runnel | tunnel |

UNSTER

| Dunster | funster | Munster | punster |

UNNY, ONY, ONEY

bunny	funny	honey	**money**
sonny	sunny	tunny	**scrimony**
agrimony	alimony	matrimony	

(And other false rhymes.)

UNTLE

frontal	disgruntle	contrapuntal

UPER, UPOR

Cupar	stupor	*(And see OOPER.)*

UPID

Cupid	stupid

UPIL, UPLE

pupil	scruple	quadruple

UPPER

crupper	scupper	*(And extend UP for "supper," etc.)*

UPPLE

couple	supple

URAL

crural	mural	neural	**plural**
rural	Ural	intramural	

URANCE

durance	assurance	endurance	**insurance**

URBAN

Durban	turban	urban	**suburban**

URBER, URBAR

curber	Durbar	disturber	**perturber**
superber			

URBISH

furbish	Serbish	superbish

URCHASED, URCHEST

purchased

(And extend EARCH, ERCH, IRCH, URCH, for "birch-est," etc.)

169

U

URDEN

burden	guerdon	Purdon	disburden
overburden			

URDER (see IRDAR, IRDER)

URDY, IRDIE

birdie	curdy	Ferdie	sturdy
wordy	hurdy-gurdy		

UREAU

bureau	Douro	Truro	futuro

URFY

Murphy	scurfy	surfy	turfy

URGENT

purgent	surgent	turgent	urgent
convergent	detergent	divergent	emergent
insurgent	resurgent		

URGEON

bourgeon	Sir John	Spurgeon	sturgeon
surgeon	habergeon		

URIOUS

curious	furious	spurious	Asturias
incurious	injurious	luxurious	penurious
usurious			

URIST, UREST

jurist	poorest	purist	tourist
caricaturist	(And extend URE for "purest," etc.)		

URKY (see ERKY)   URLY (see EARLY)

URLEW

curlew	purlieu

URMOIL

sperm-oil	turmoil

URMUR (see IRMER)   URNER (see EARNER)

URNET

burnet	gurnet	ternate	alternate

170

URNISH

burnish	furnish	sternish

UROR

furor	juror

(And extend OOR and URE for "poorer," "surer," etc.)

URRET

turret	"worrit"

URRIER

currier	furrier	hurrier	skurrier
spurrier	worrier		

URROW

burrow	furrow	*(Compare OROUGH.)*

URRY

curry	flurry	furry	hurry
Murray	skurry	Surrey	urry
worry			

URSAR, URSER *(see ERCER)*

URTAIN *(see ERTAIN)*

URTLE *(see IRTLE)*, URVEY

purvey	survey

URY, EWRY, OORY

brewery	Drury	ewry	fury
Newry	houri	Jewry	jury
moory	Missouri		

USCLE, USSEL, USTLE

bustle	Brussels *(for plurals)*	hustle
muscle	mussel	Russell	rustle
tussle	corpuscle		

USHER, USSIA

Prussia	Russia	usher	*(And extend USH.)*

USHY *(as in "brushy")*

brushy	cushy	gushy	lushy
mushy	plushy	rushy	

USHY *(as in "bushy")*

Bushey	bushy	wushy	pushy

171

USION

fusion	allusion	collusion	conclusion
confusion	contusion	delusion	diffusion
effusion	elusion	exclusion	extrusion
illusion	inclusion	infusion	intrusion
obtrusion	obtusion	pertusion	profusion
protusion	suffusion	transfusion	circumfusion

USKY

busky	dusky	husky	musky
tusky			

USSET

gusset	russet

USSIAN

Prussian	Russian	concussion	discussion
percussion	repercussion		

USSY

fussy	Gussie	hussy	pussy
"lawk-a-mussy"			

USTARD

bustard	custard	mustard

(And extend USTER for "blustered," etc.)

USTER

luster	muster

(And extend UST for "duster," "robuster" etc.)

USTFUL

lustful	trustful	disgustful	distrustful
mistrustful			

USTIAN

fustian	combustion

USTIC

fustic	rustic

USTINGS

hustings   *(And extend UST for "dustings," etc.)*

USTLE (see USCLE)

USTOM

custom	frustum	accustom

USTY

fusty	lusty	musty

(And extend UST for "dusty," etc.)

USY (see IZZY)   UTAL (see OOTLE)

UTHFUL

ruthful	toothful	truthful	youthful
untruthful			

UTILE

futile	utile	inutile

UTION

ablution	absolution	allocution	attribution
circumlocution	circumvolution	collocution	consecution
constitution	contribution	convolution	dilution
destitution	devolution	diminution	dissolution
distribution	elocution	evolution	execution
institution	interlocution	involution	irresolution
Lilliputian	persecution	pollution	prosecution
prostitution	resolution	restitution	retribution
revolution	solution	substitution	volution

UTLER

butler	cutler	scuttler	subtler
sutler			

UTNEY

chutney	Putney	gluttony	muttony

UTON

Luton	Newton	Teuton

UTTER

butter	clutter	cutter	flutter
gutter	mutter	putter	shutter
splutter	sputter	stutter	strutter
utter	Calcutta	rebutter	

UTTLE

buttle	cuttle	scuttle	shuttle
subtle			

UTTOCK

buttock	futtock	puttock

UTTON

button	Dutton	glutton	mutton
Sutton	unbutton		

UTTY

putty	puttee	tutty

(And extend UT for "cutty," etc.)

UTY (see OOTY)

UVIAL

pluvial	alluvial

UXION (see UCTION)   UYER (see IAR)

UZZLE

guzzle	muzzle	nuzzle	puzzle

UZZY

buzzy	fuzzy	hussy	muzzy
Fuzzy-Wuzzy			

U

	YCLE		
cycle	Michael	Lake Baikal	
	YLON		
nylon	pylon		
	YMEN		
hymen	flymen (*stage*)	piemen	Simon
	YNTAX		
syntax	tin-tacks		
	YPTIC		
cryptic	styptic	elliptic	
	YPIST		
typist	(*And extend* IPE *for* "ripest," *etc.*)		
	YTHAM		
lytham	rhythm	Witham